AF327101

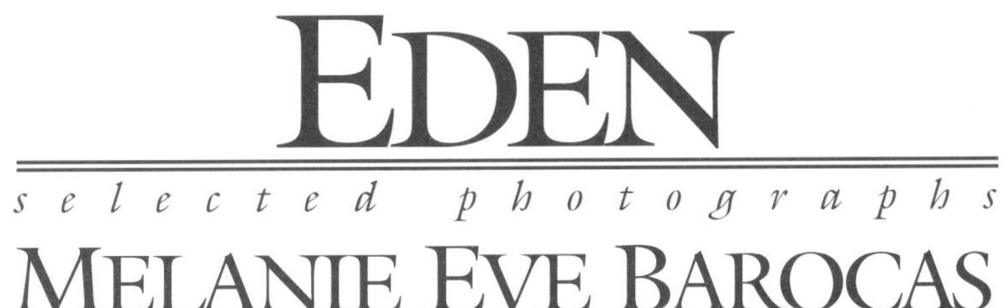

# EDEN

*selected photographs*

## MELANIE EVE BAROCAS

Eve Editions

ACKNOWLEDGMENTS

*To John Philion for years of helping me design.*

*To Gina Marsh for helping me scan the rough draft.*

*To Van Dyck Press, Ltd for pursuing quality.*

*Most of all to the people who, for a moment,
welcomed me into their world.*

# EDEN

EDEN, this house in which we dwell each day
without suspecting our gift of paradise
and through which we make our solitary way.
If it is true that heaven is bliss and hell is misery
with earth between the two,
then this home we inhabit is both one and the other.

Only we can choose to make heaven of hell
or hell of heaven.

*Melanie Eve Barocas*

INSTITUTE FOR DEAF CHILDREN
PORT-AU-PRINCE, HAITI

1

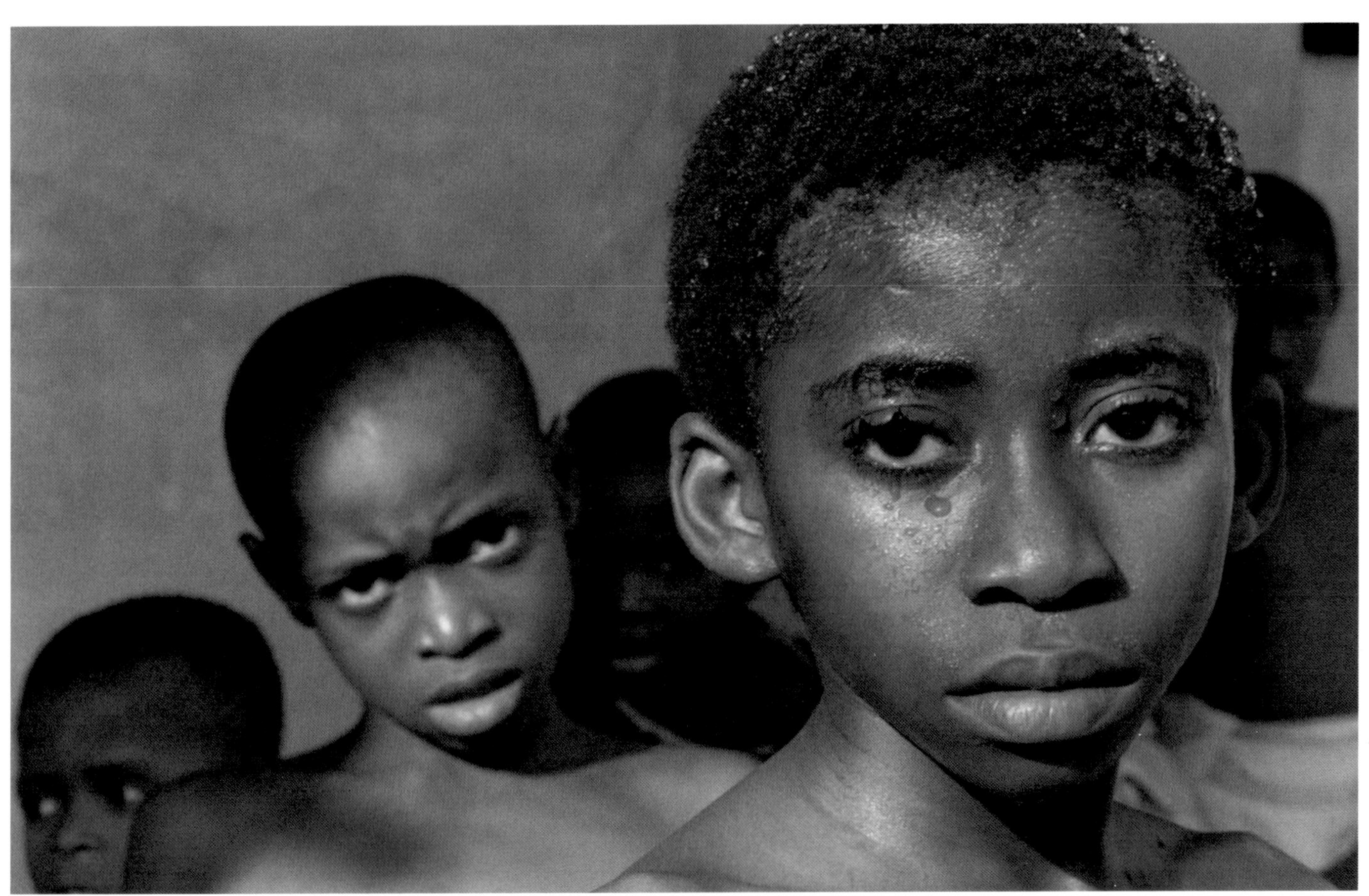

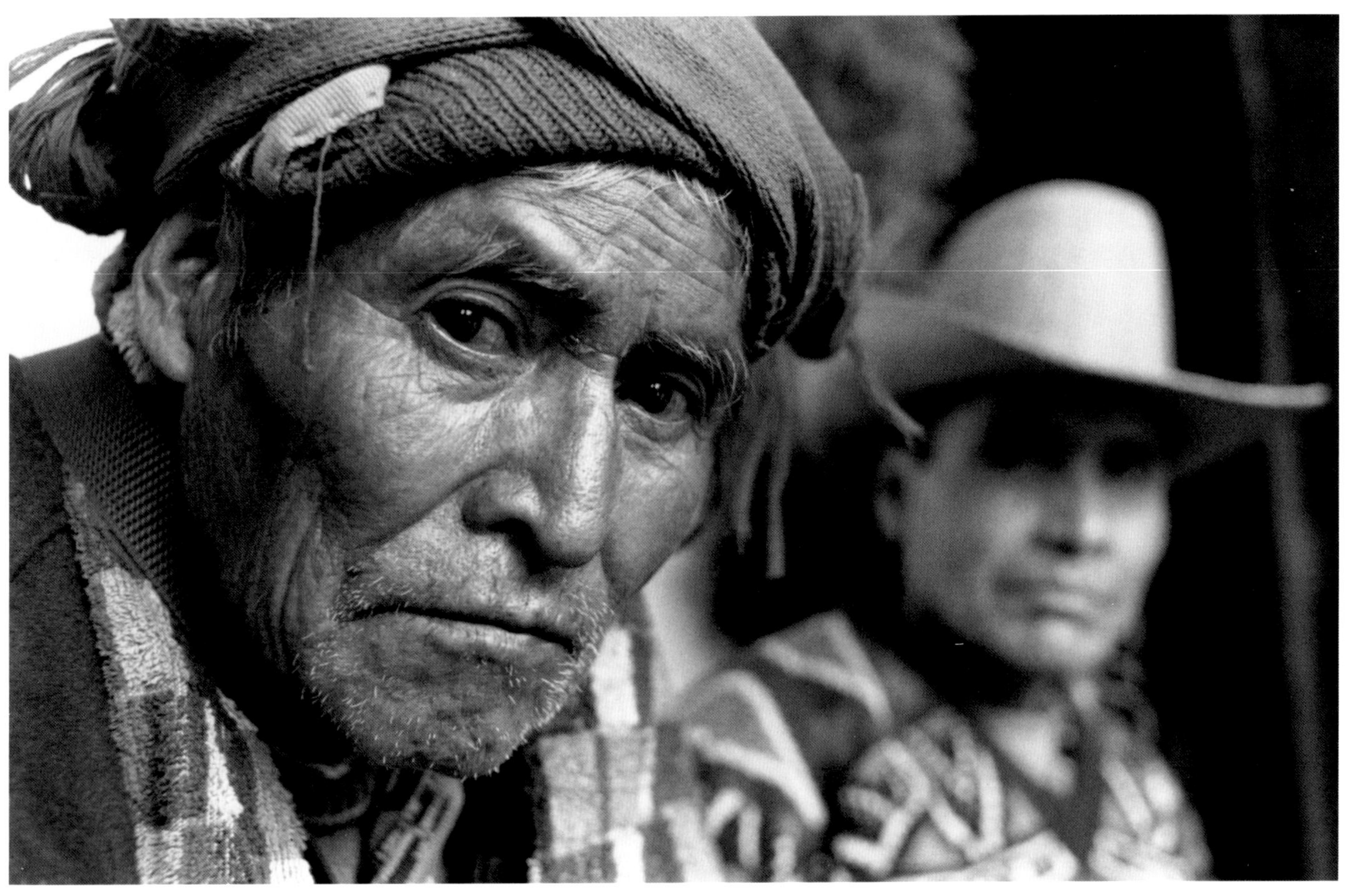

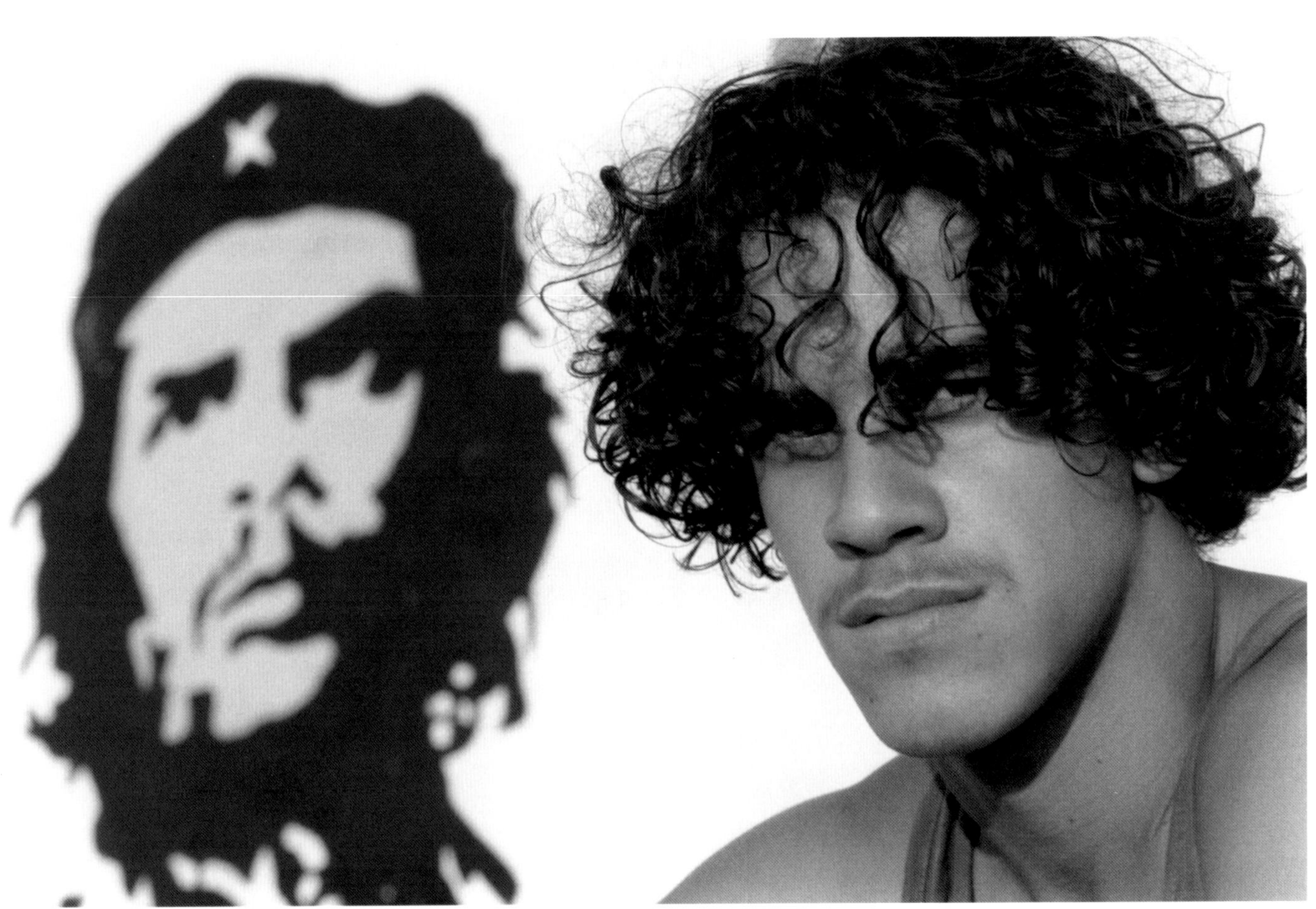

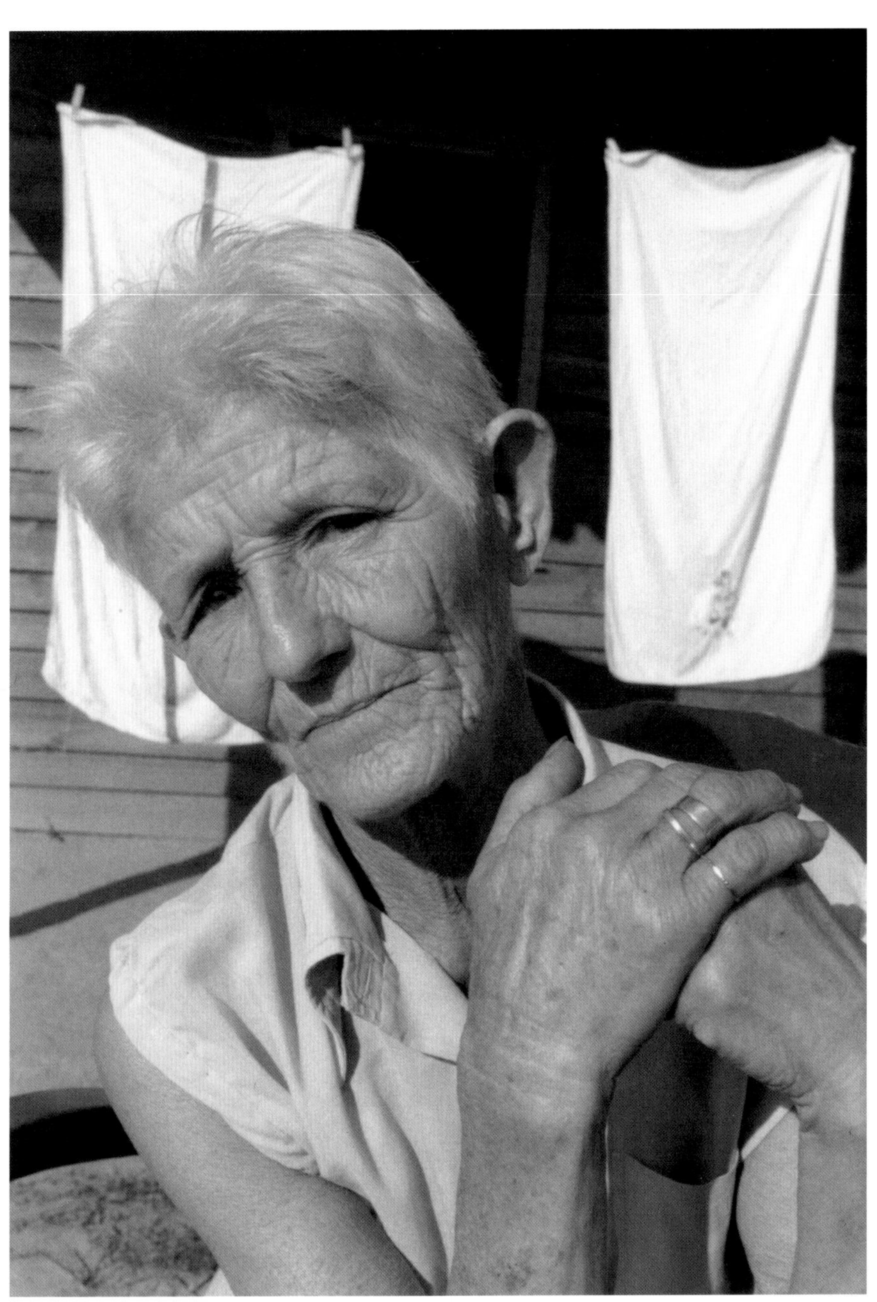

LONNIE RAY
DETROIT, MICHIGAN

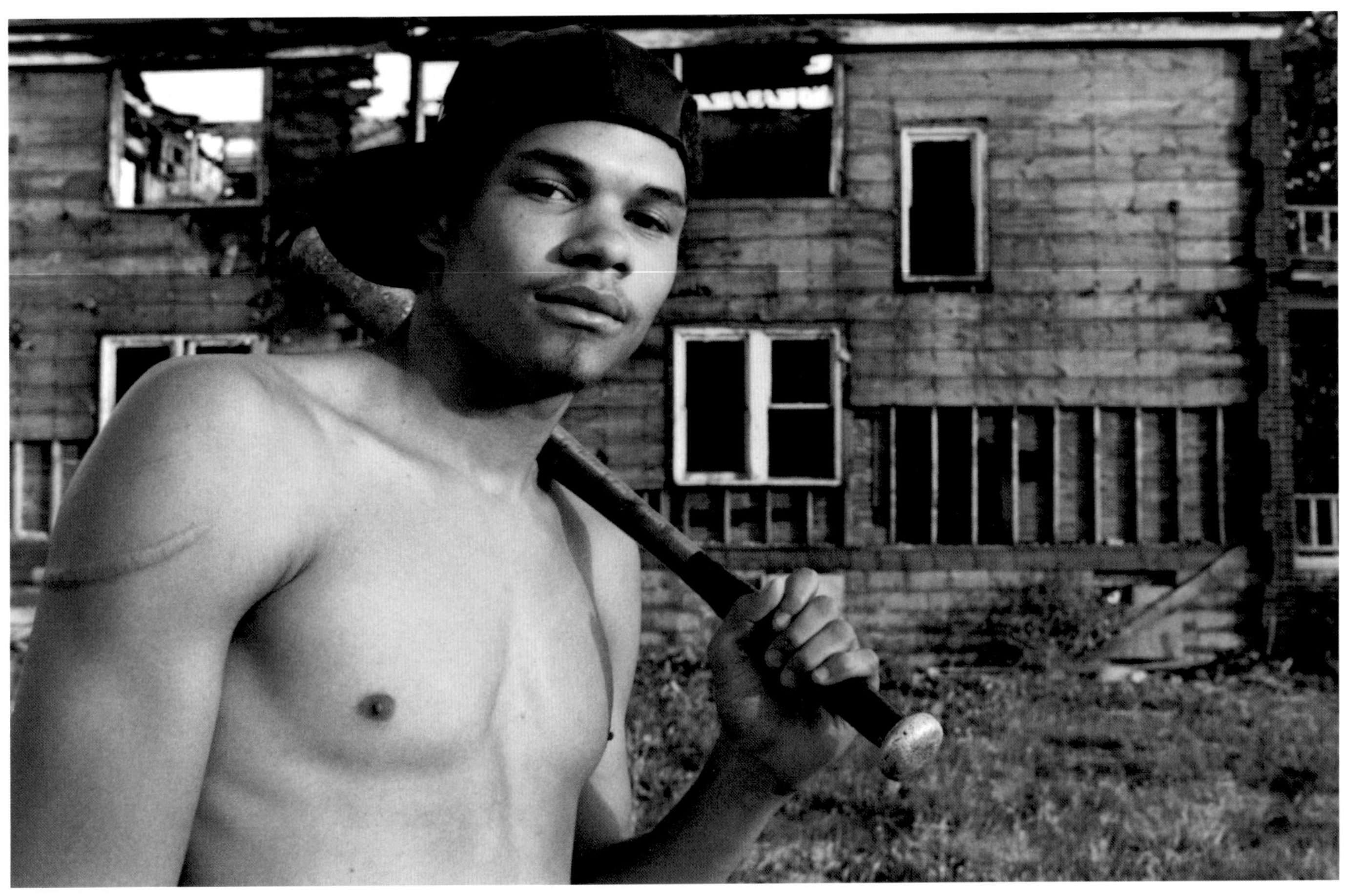

ASHTA, INDIA

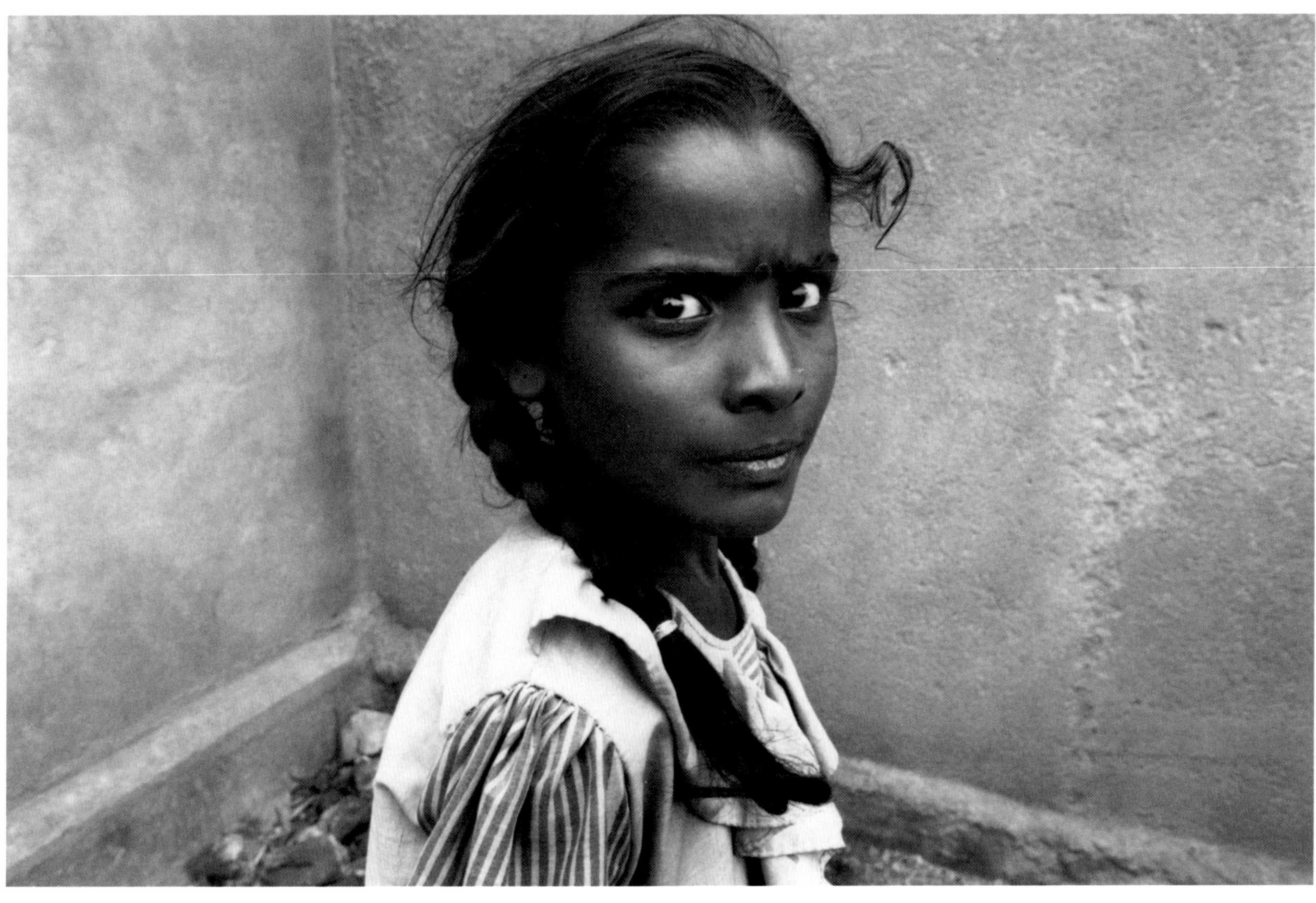

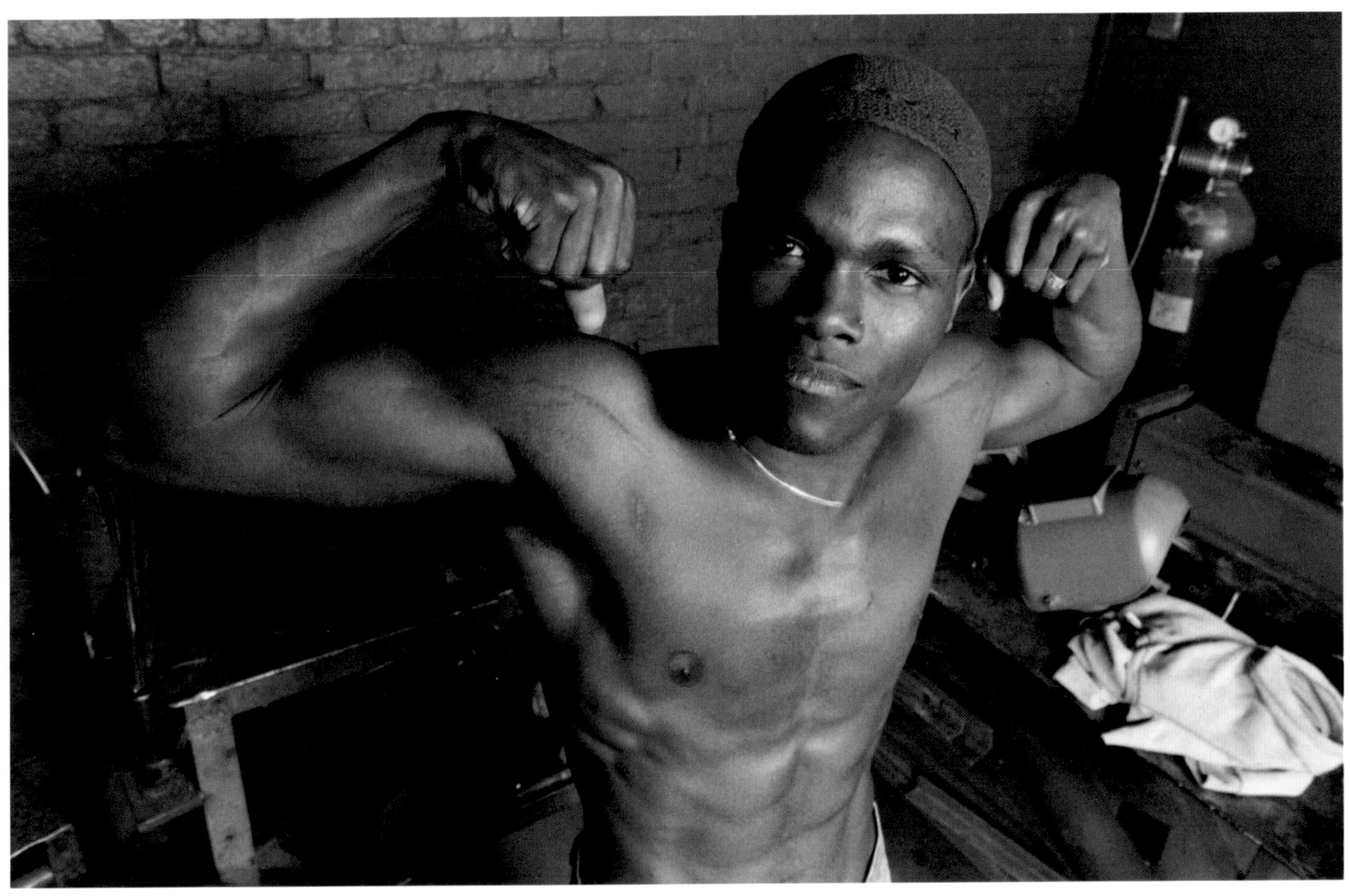

SOMALIA-KENYA BORDER

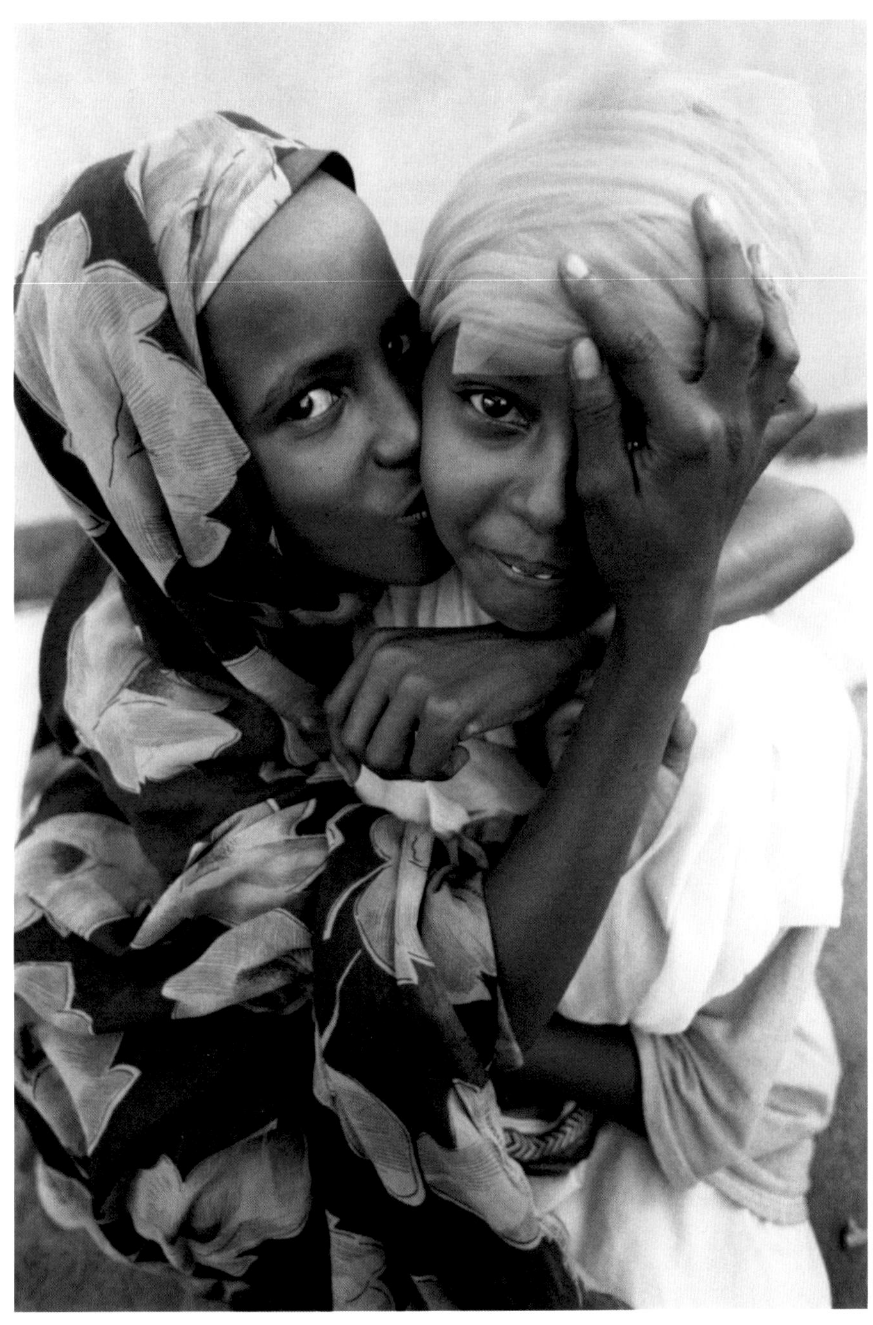

DILLON
TAOS, NEW MEXICO

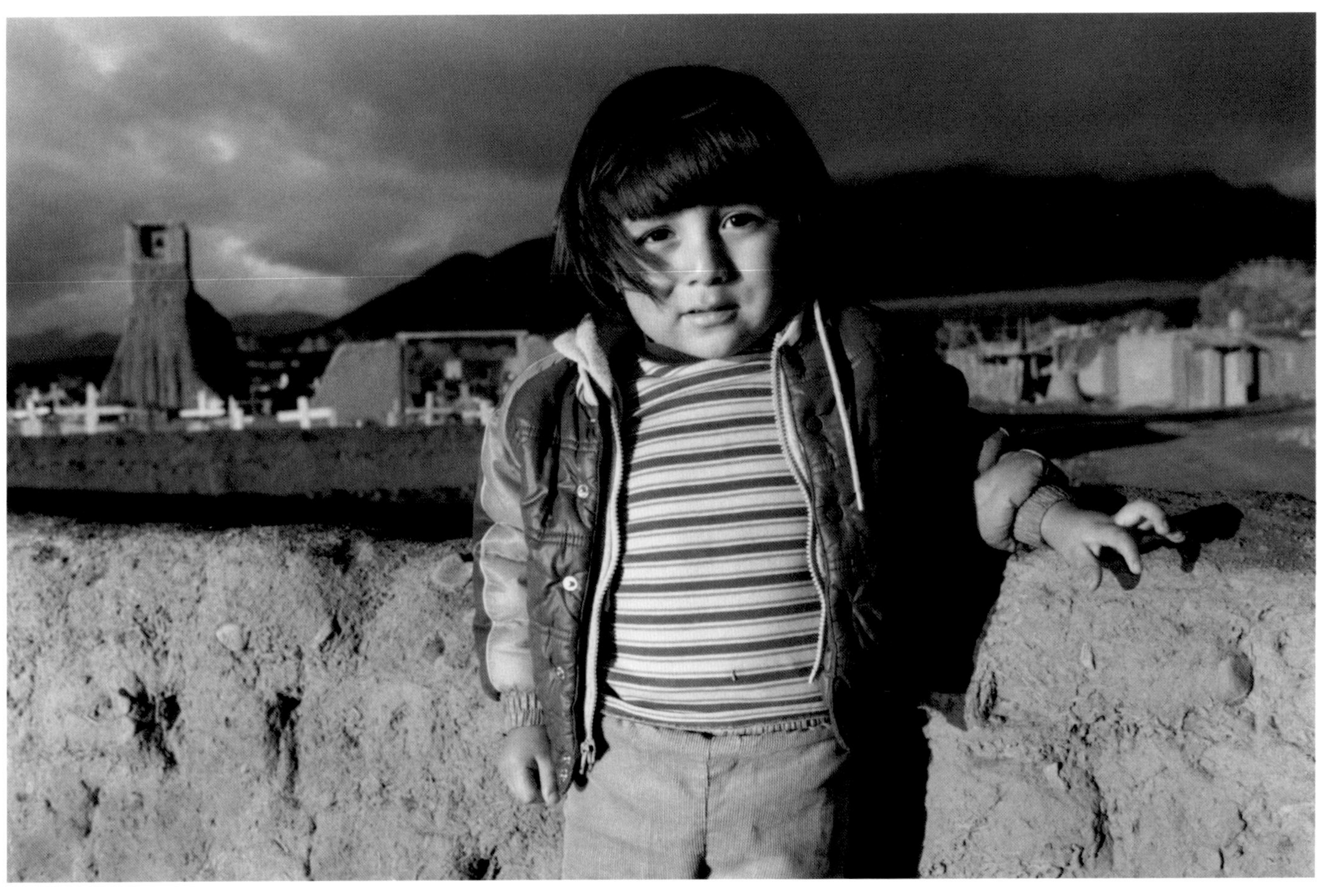

HAZEL
LA GRANGE, ARKANSAS

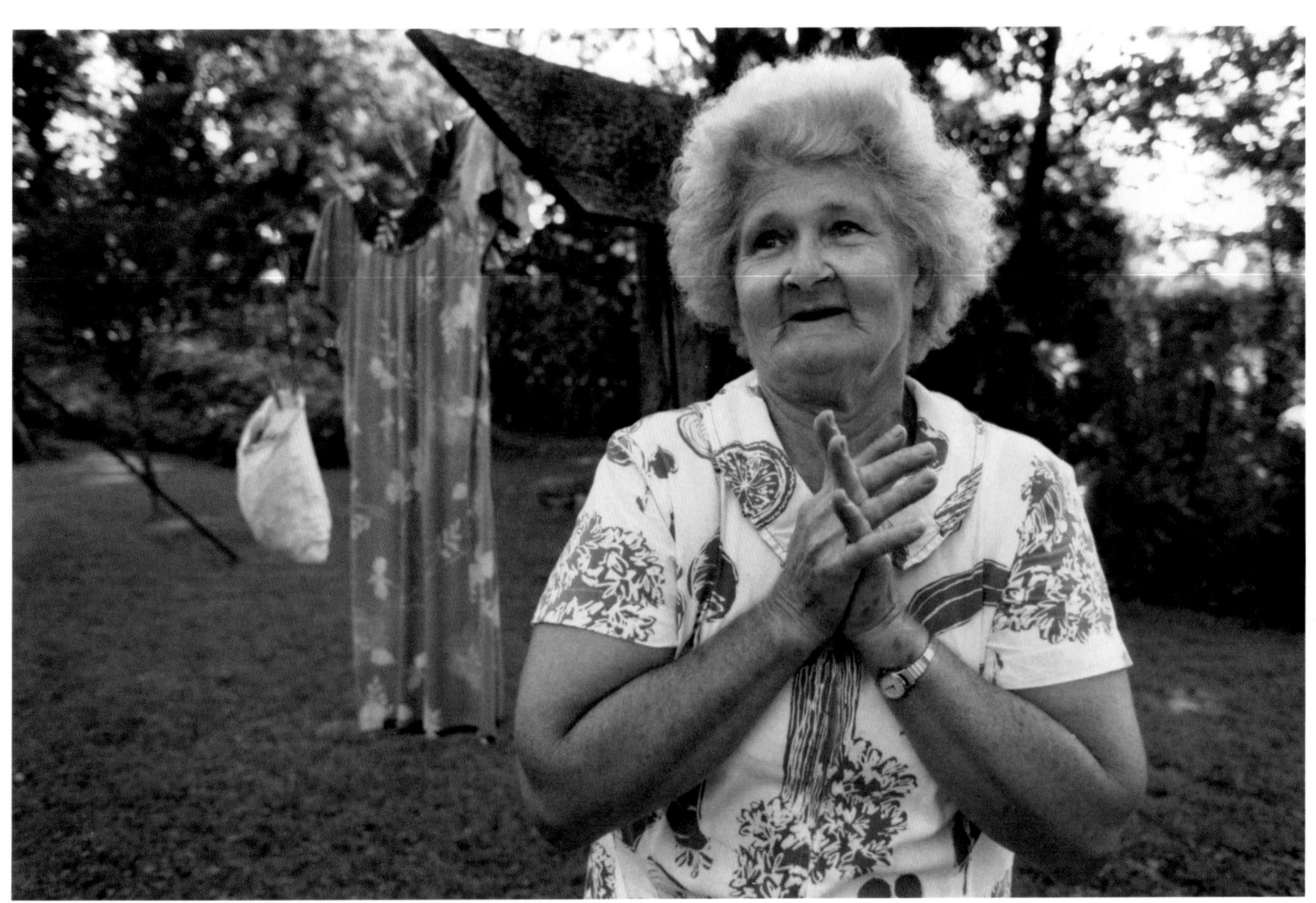

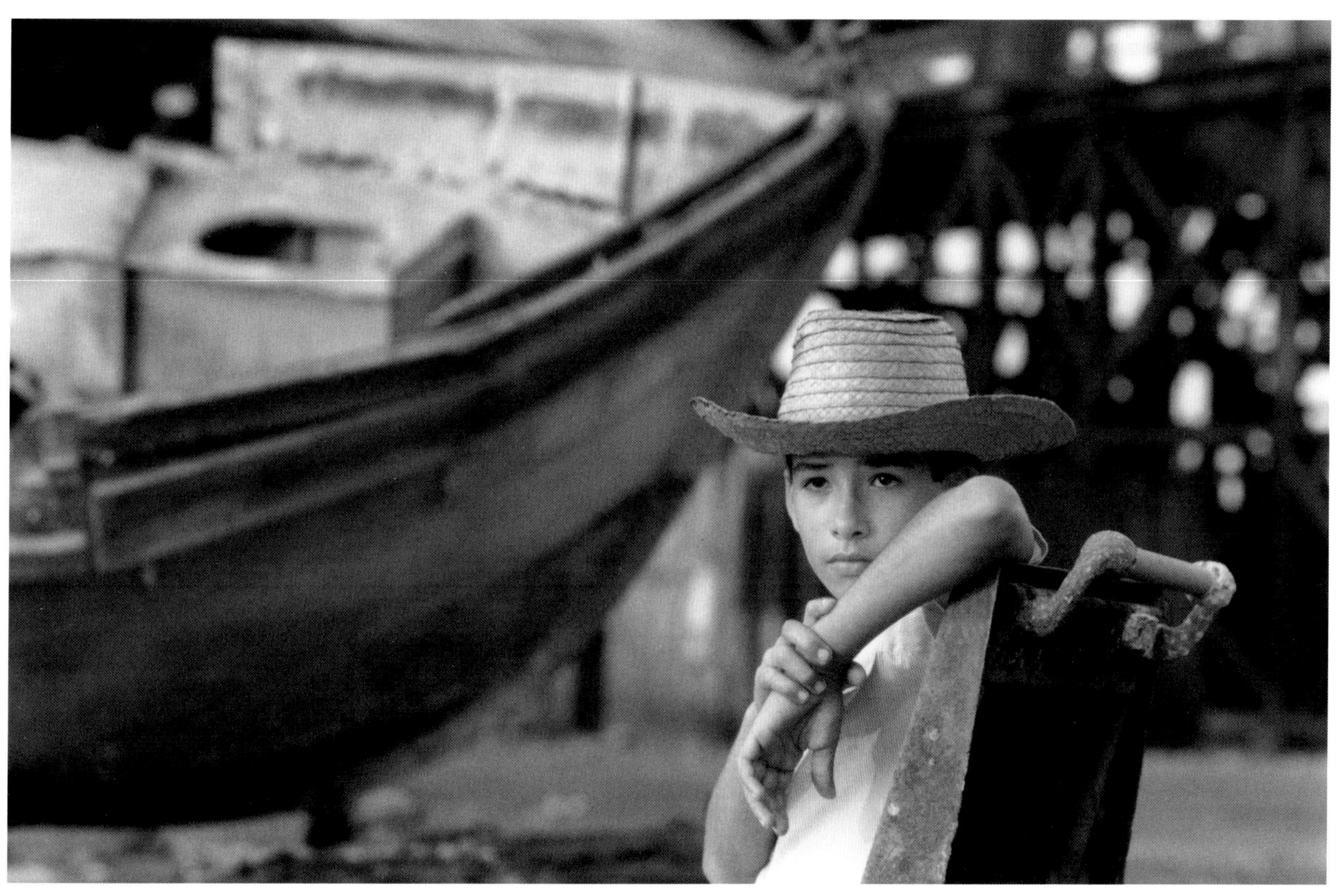

Margaret & Patrick
New Ross, Ireland

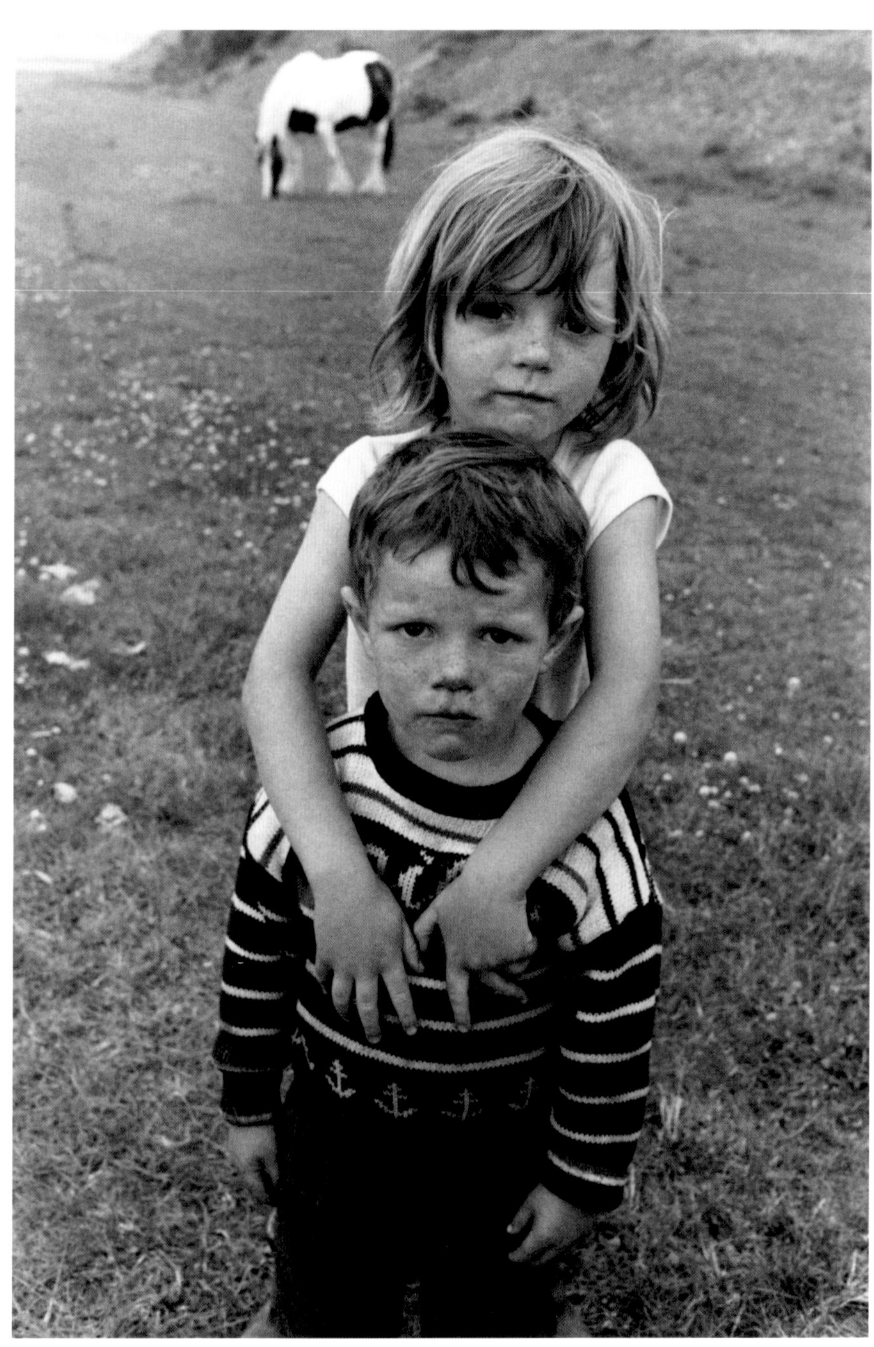

MANAGUA, NICARAGUA

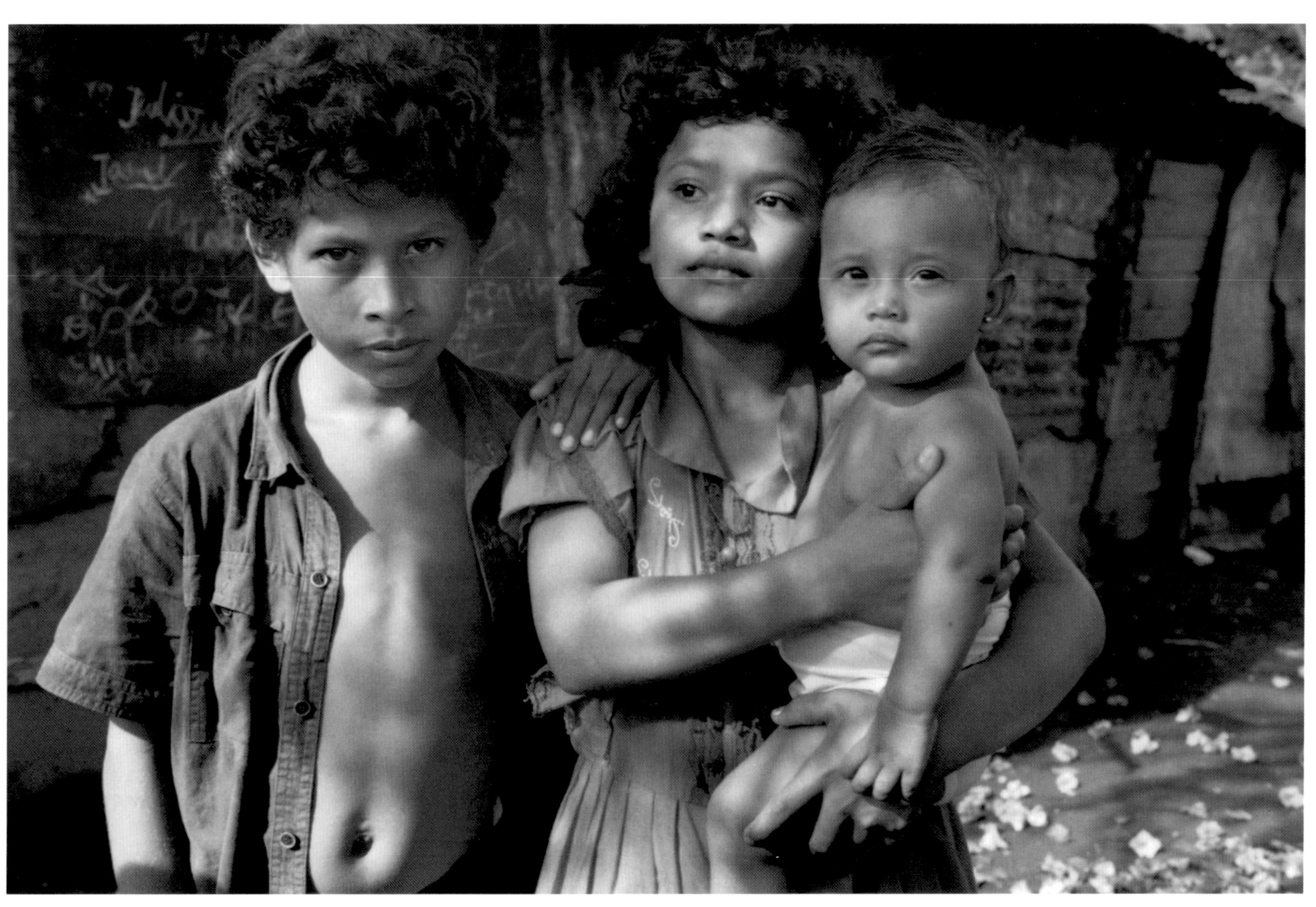

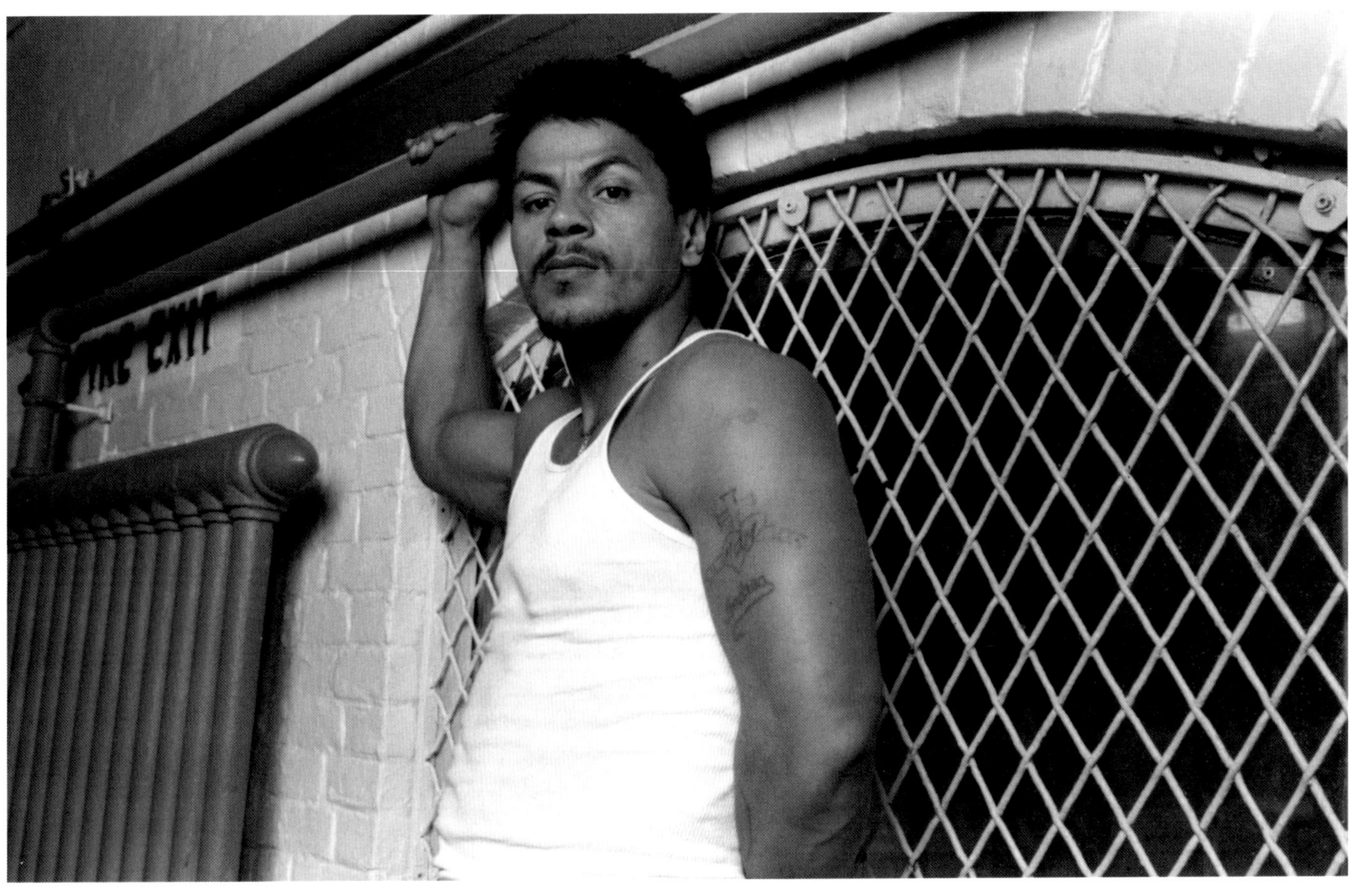

FIRE EXIT

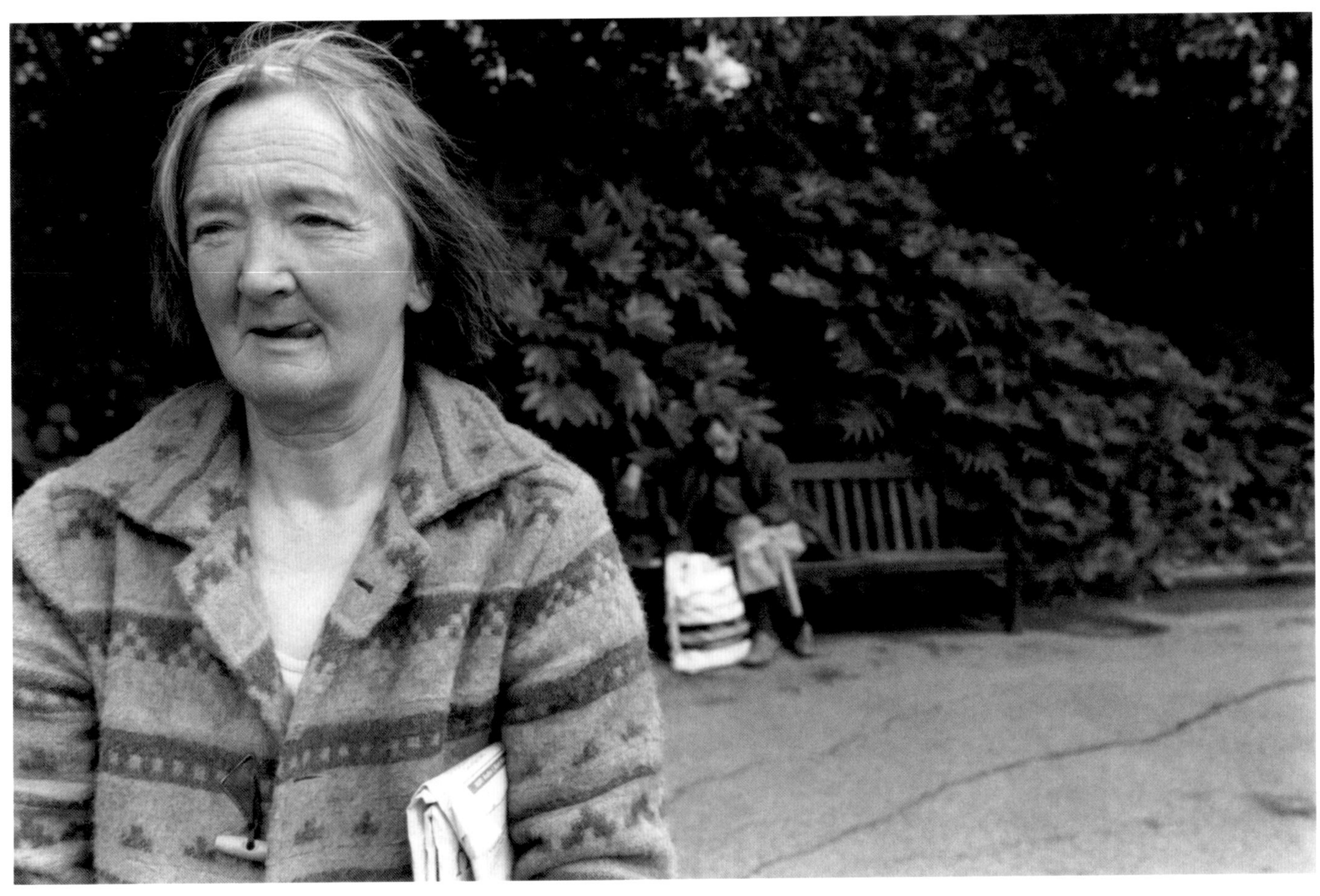

JIM
PROTESTANT BELFAST, IRELAND

16

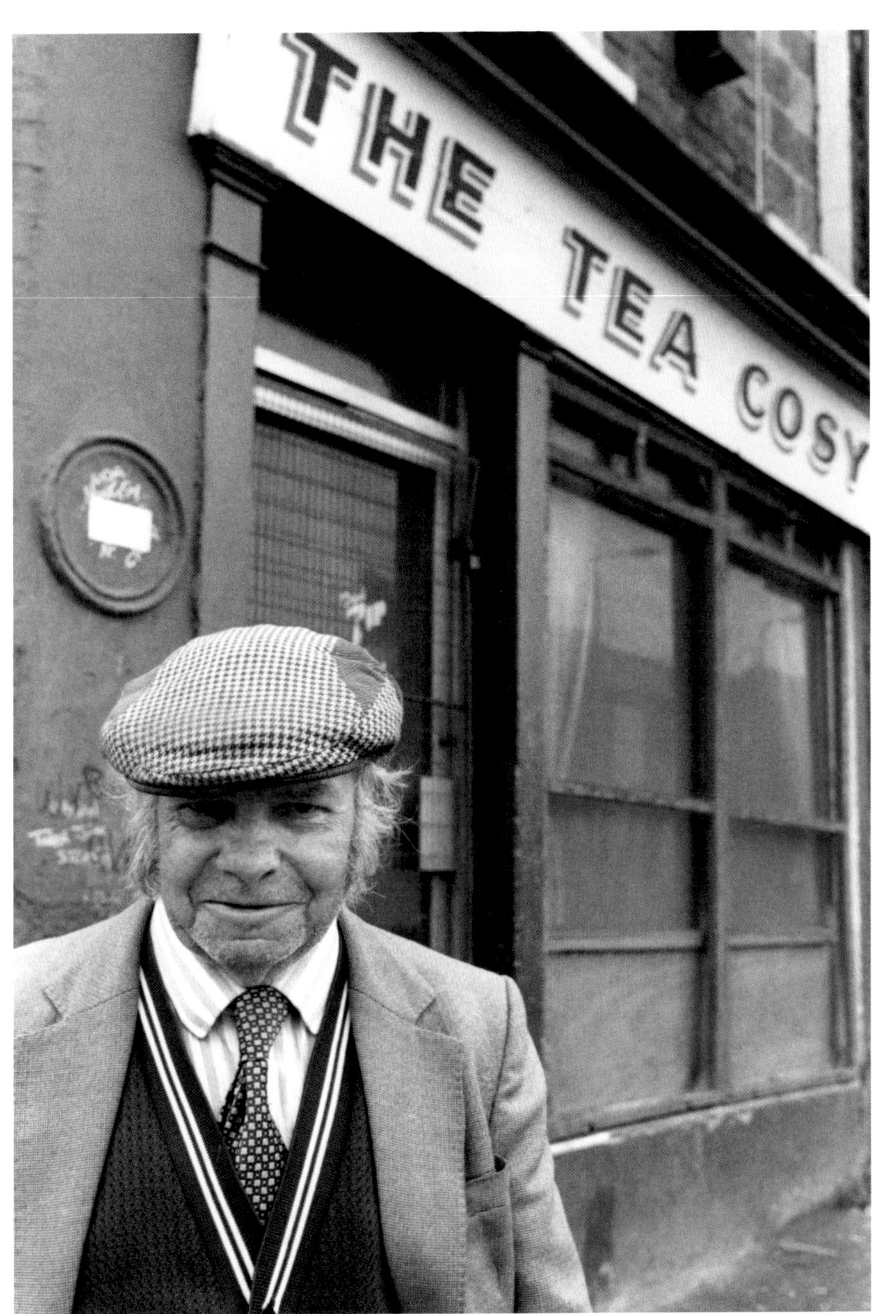

THE TEA COSY

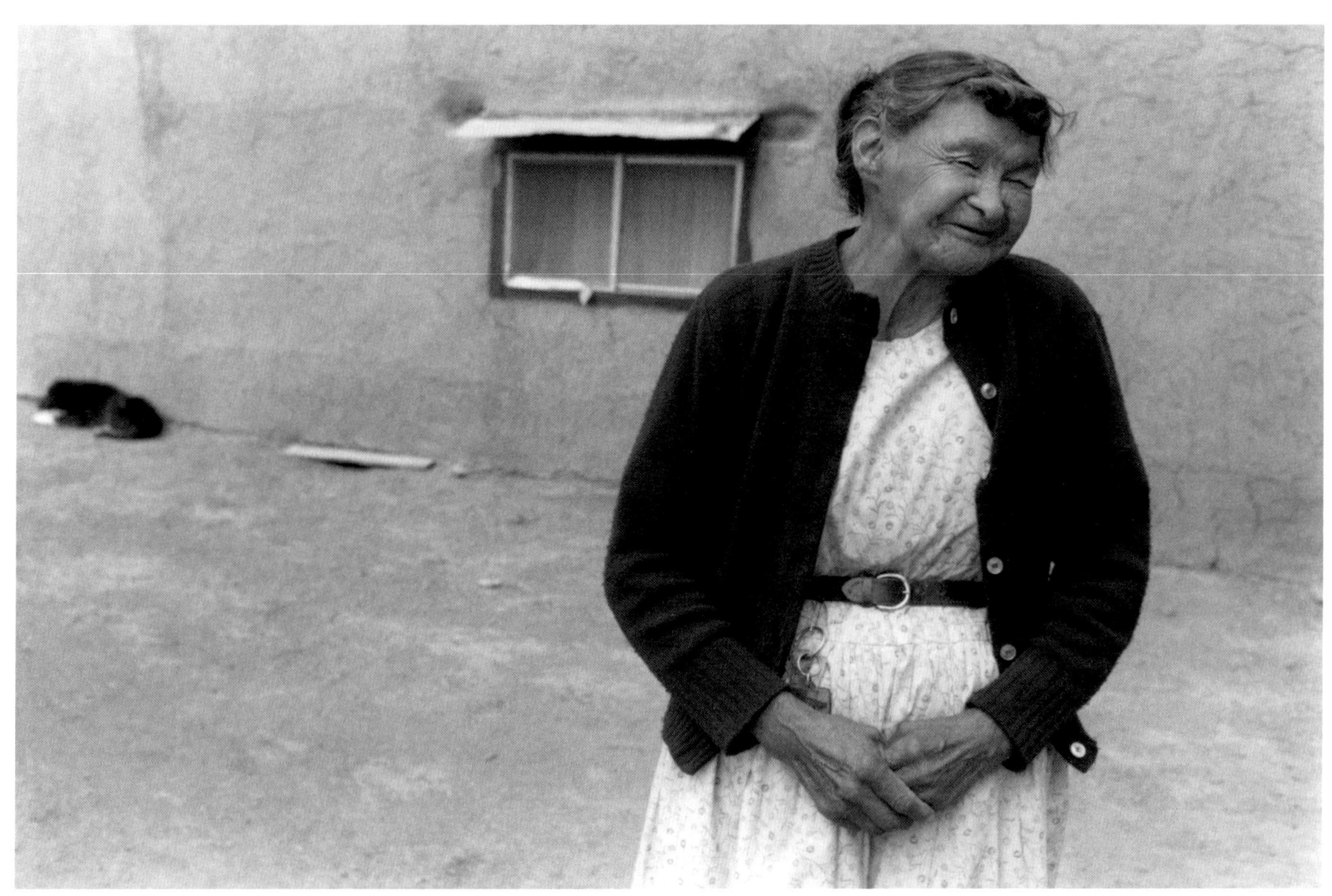

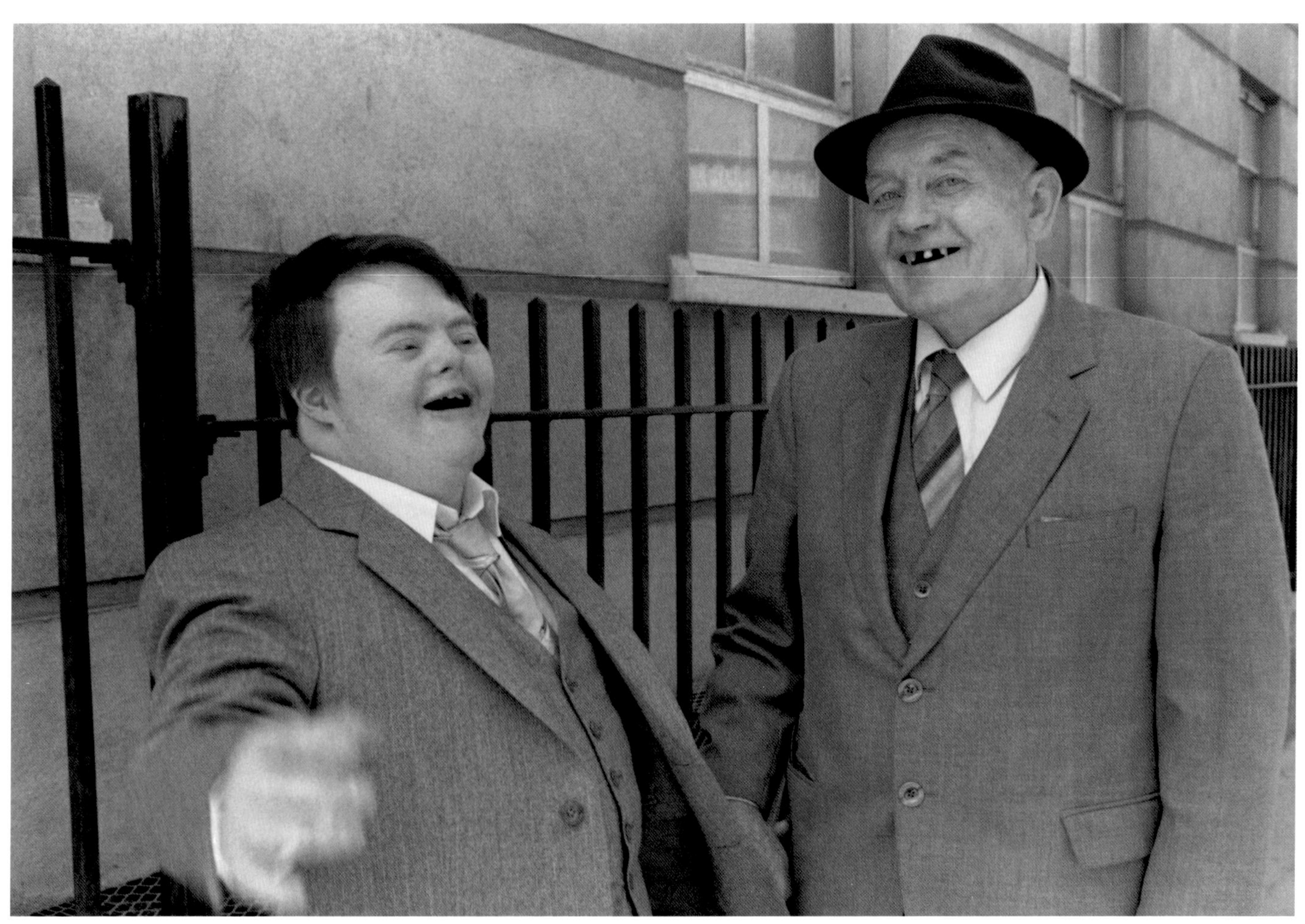

DEACON EDDIE RICE
HETH, ARKANSAS

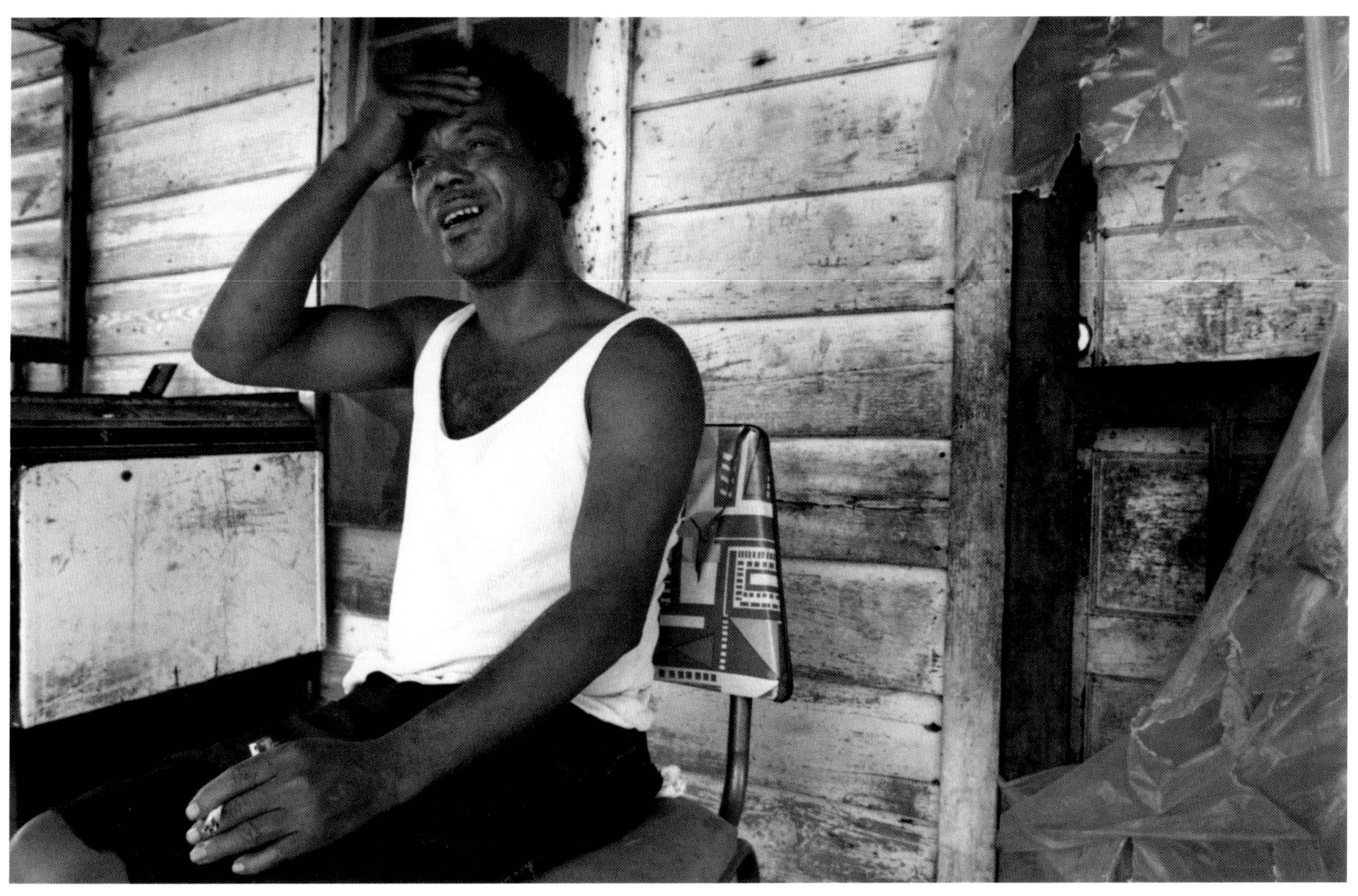

MOHAMED
SOMALIA-KENYA BORDER

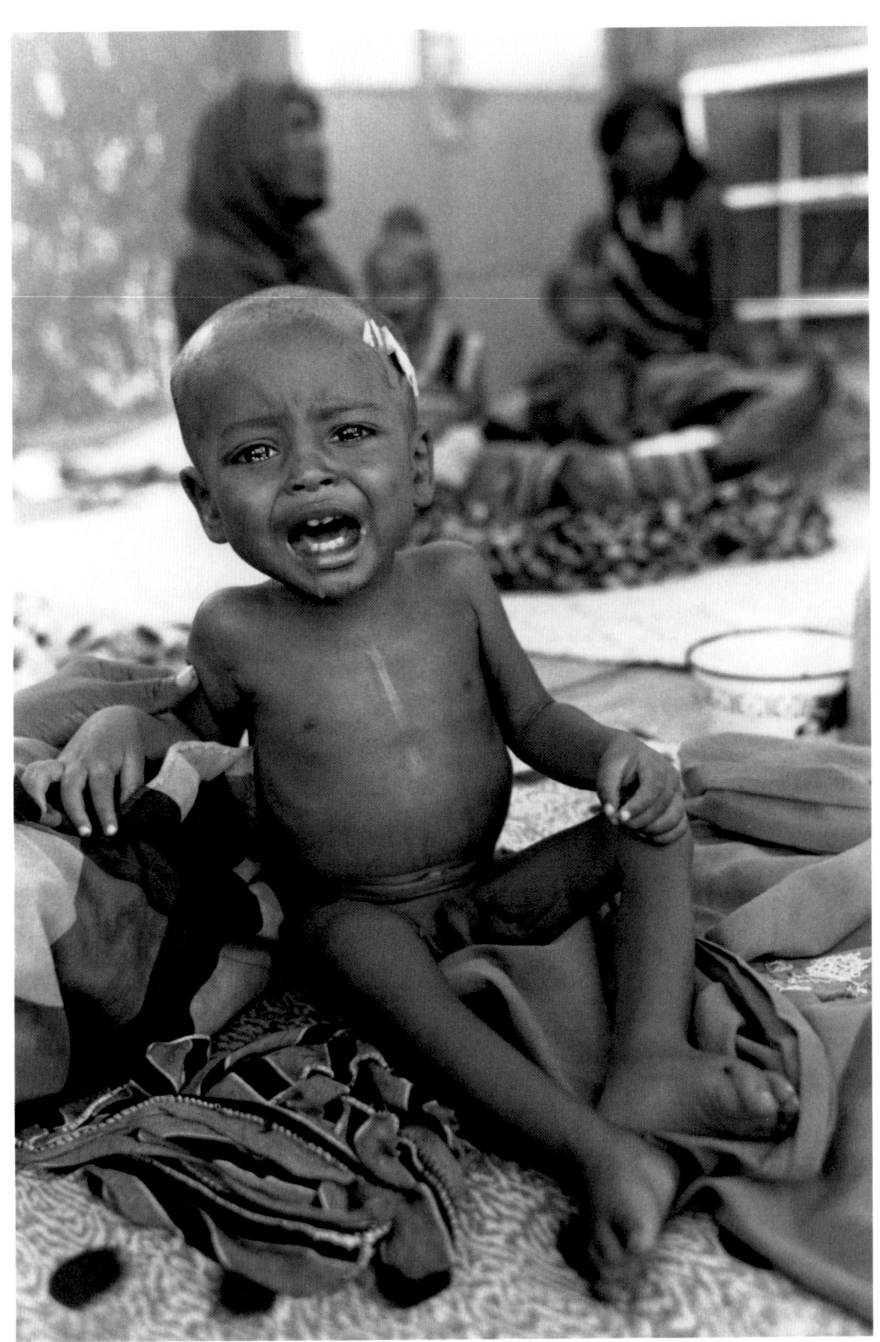

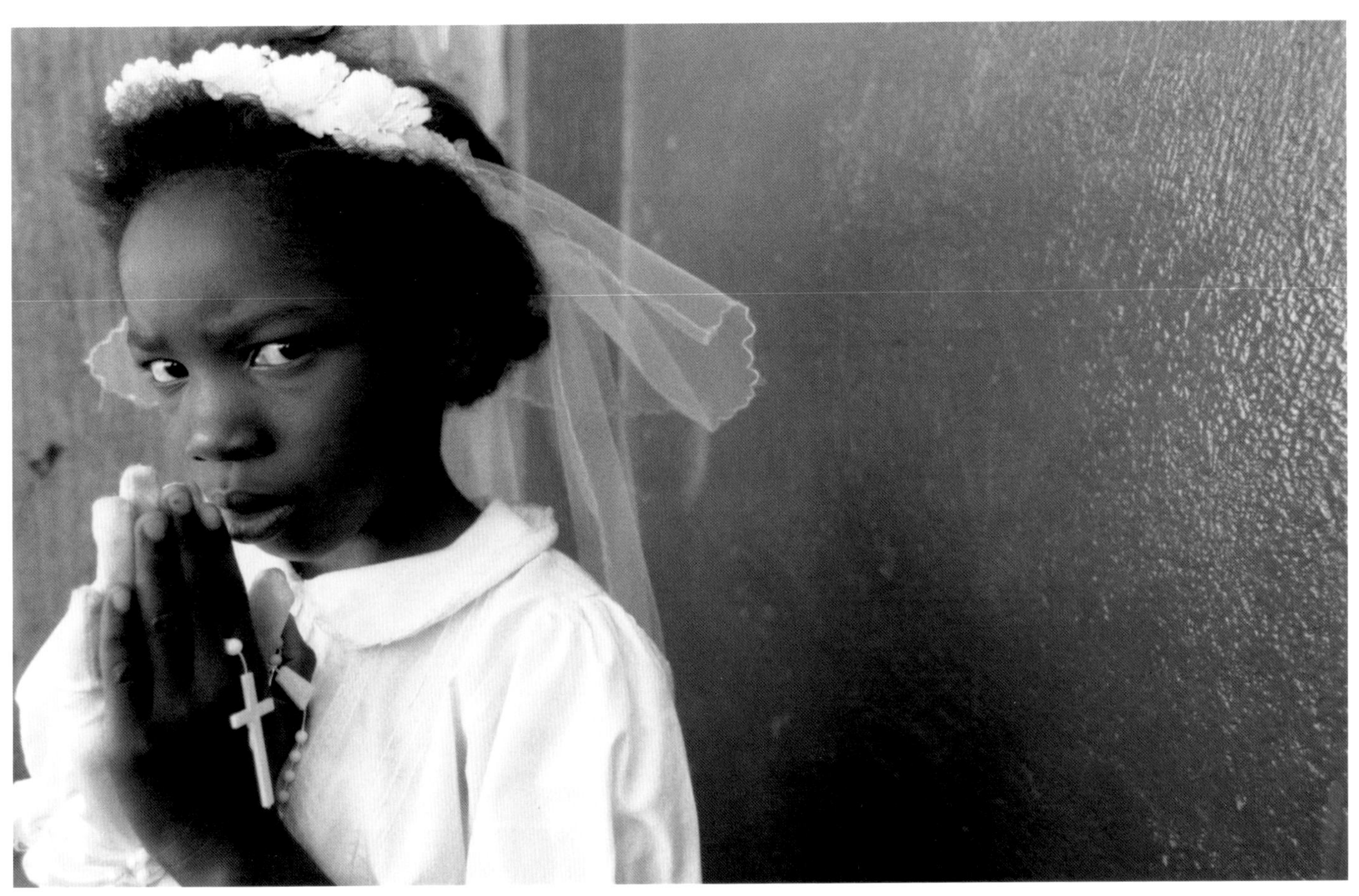

Beijing, China

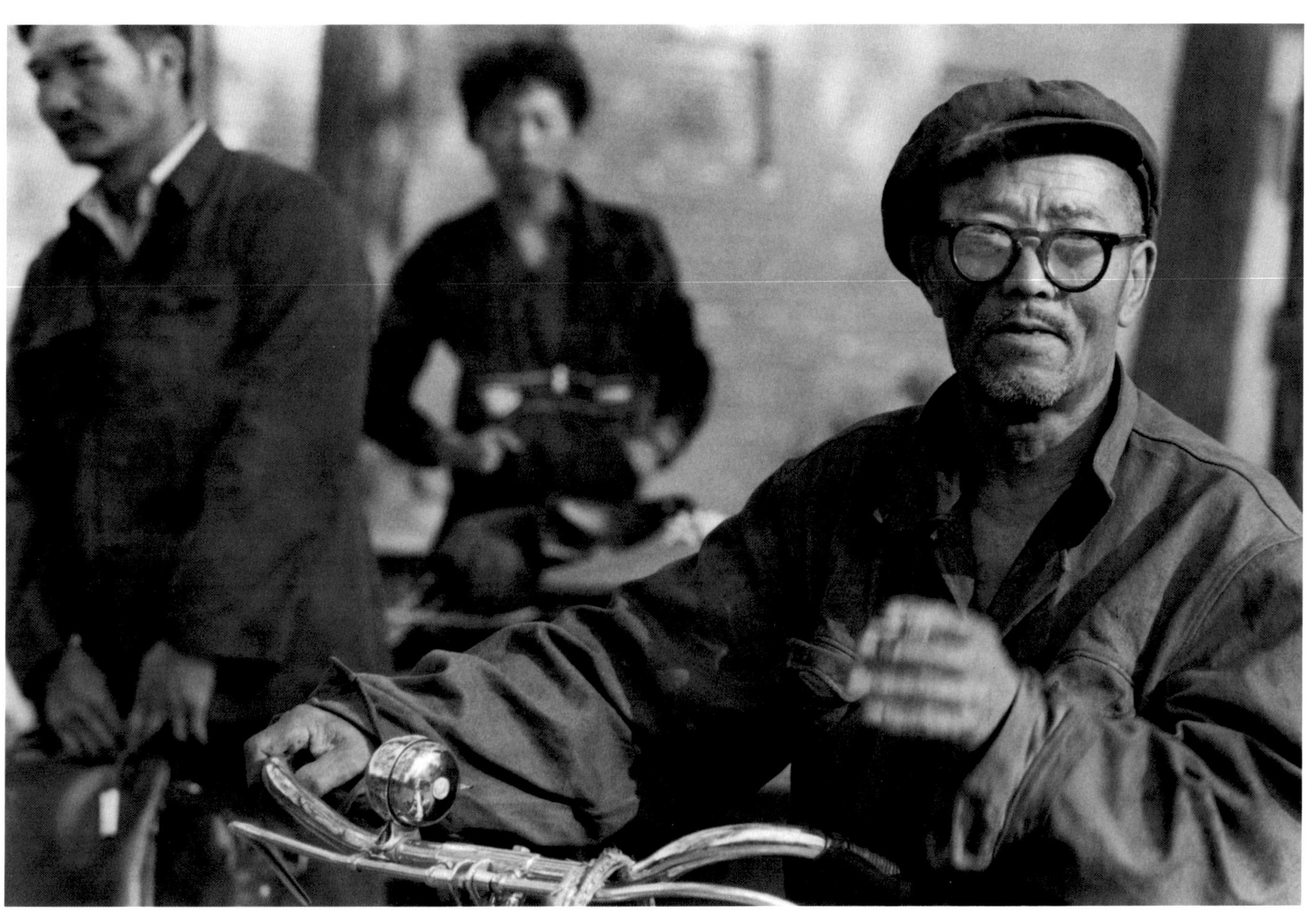

MARLIN
HELENA, ARKANSAS

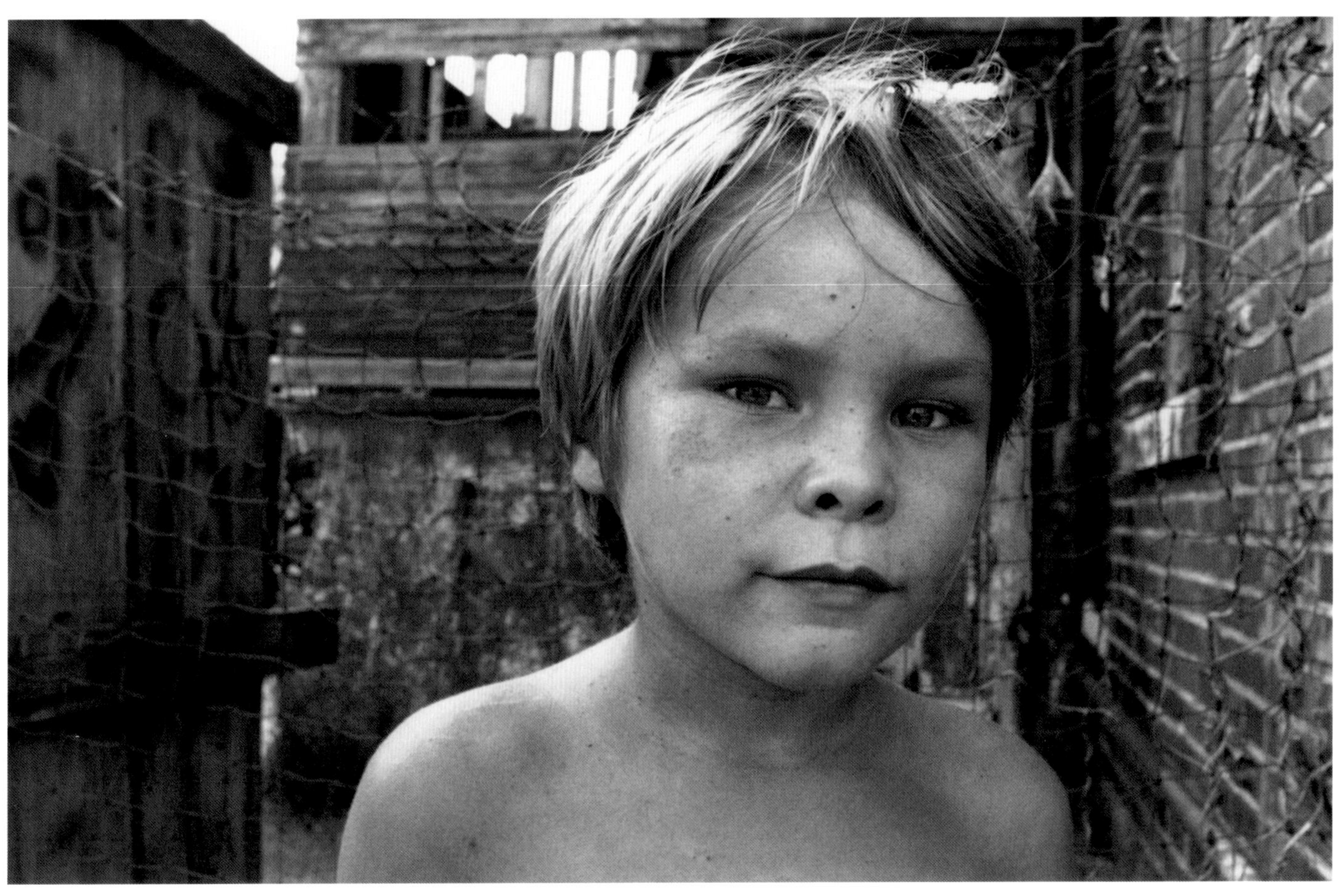

SHANGHAI, CHINA

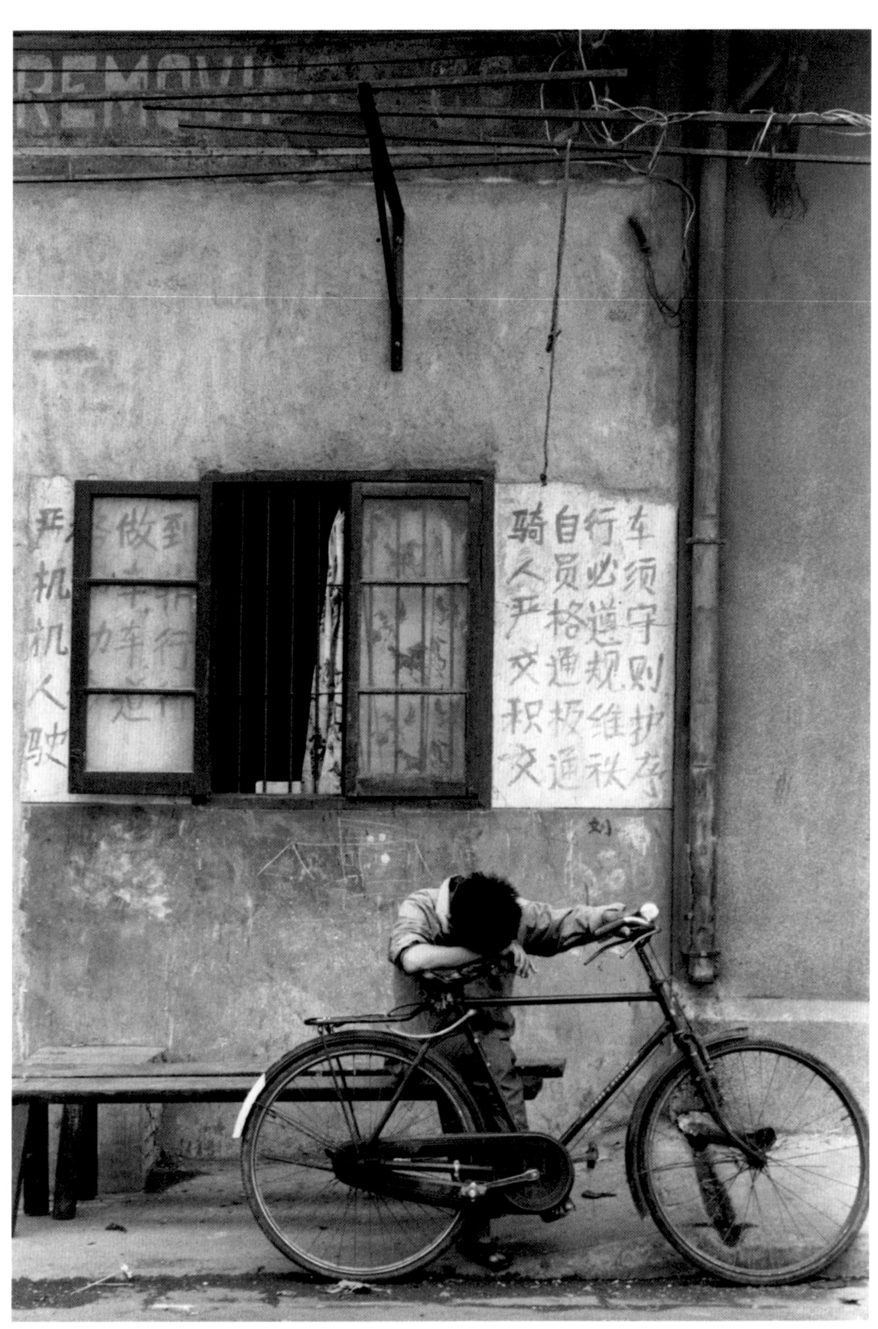
骑自行车
人员必须
严格遵守
交通规则
积极维护
交通秩序
严格做到
机动车行
机动车速
人驶

BOBBY & BOBBY JR
EUDORA, ARKANSAS

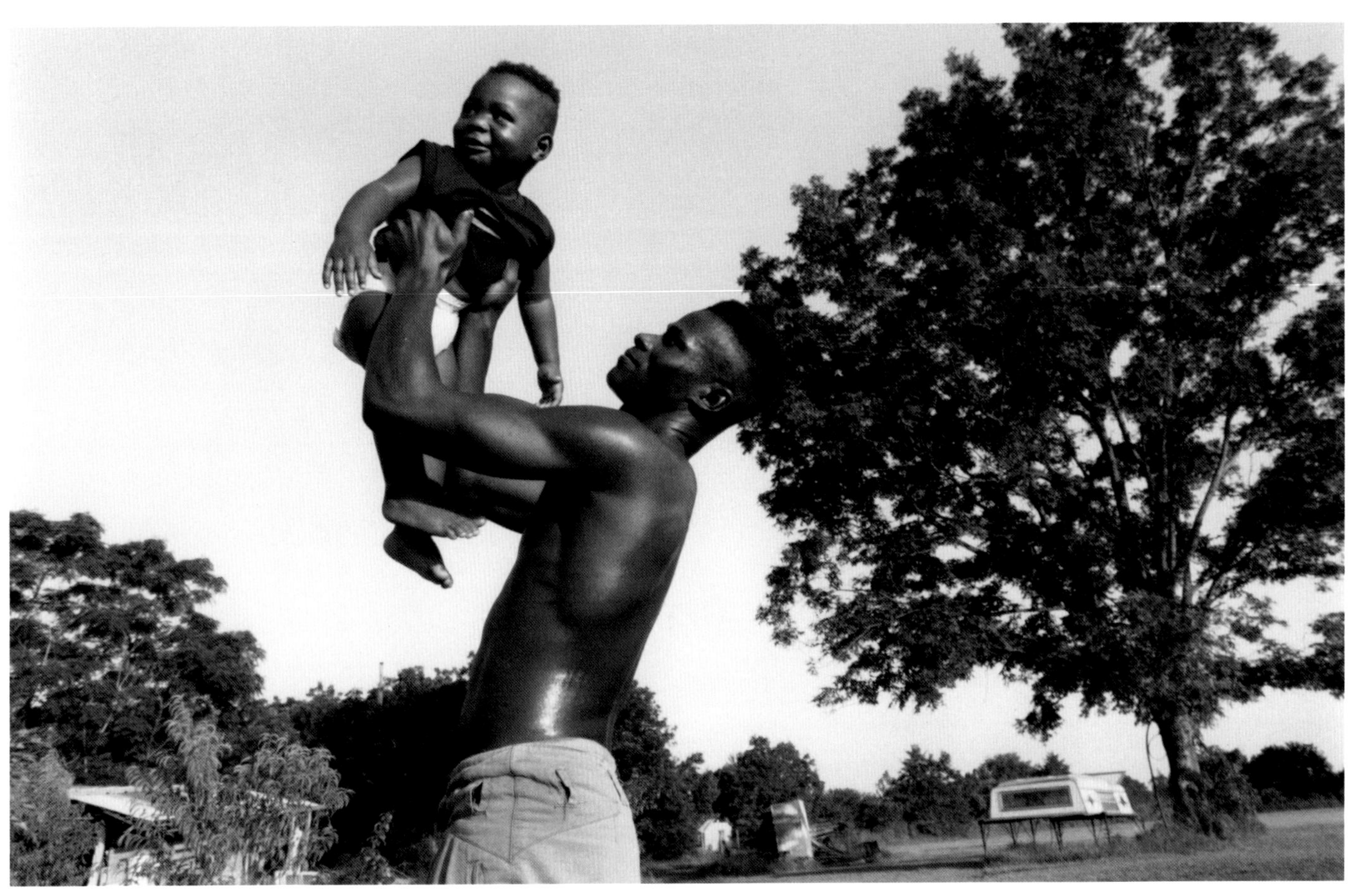

MALNUTRITION
SAINT HELENE, HAITI

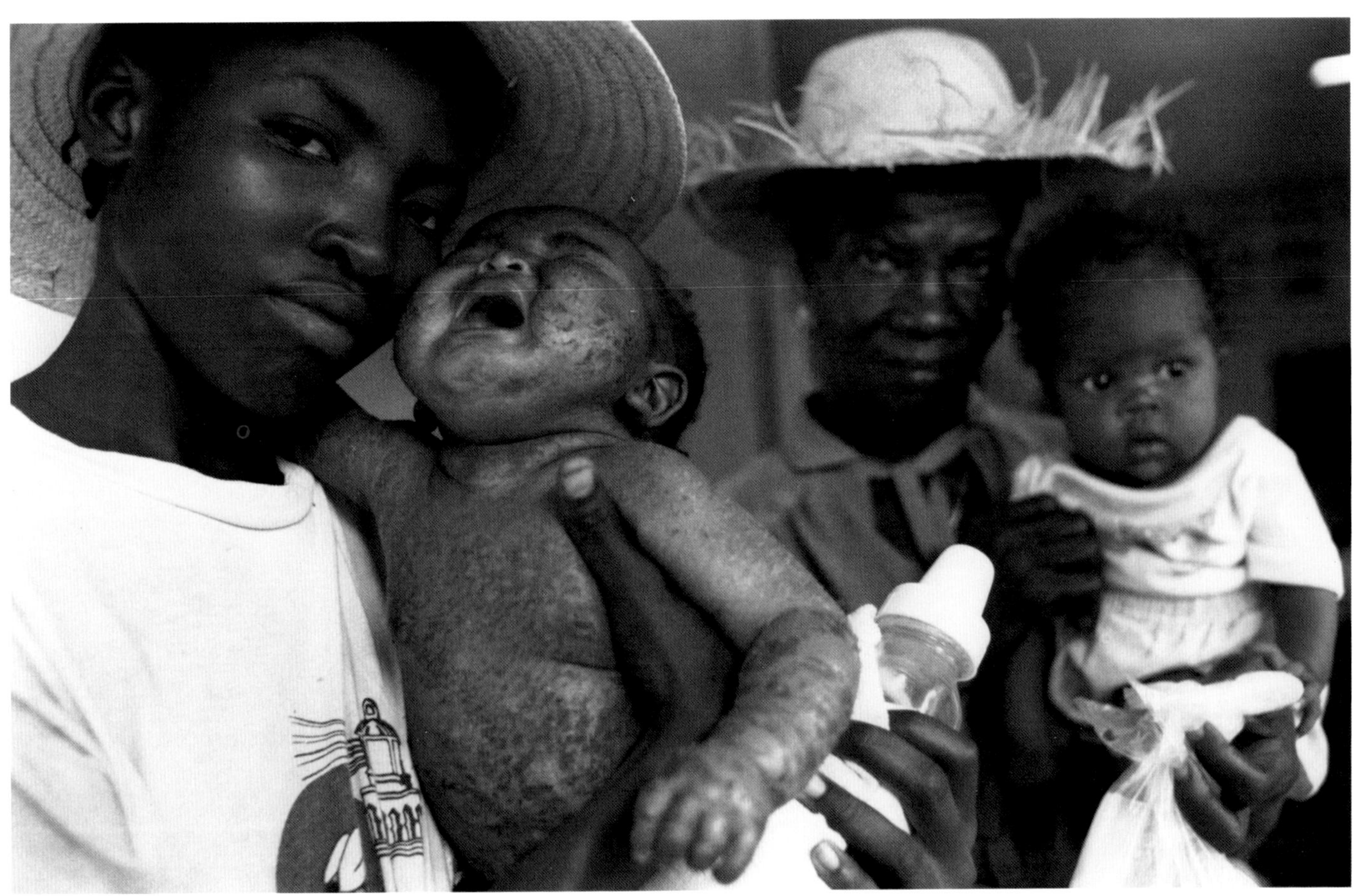

ROAD TO BOMBAY, INDIA

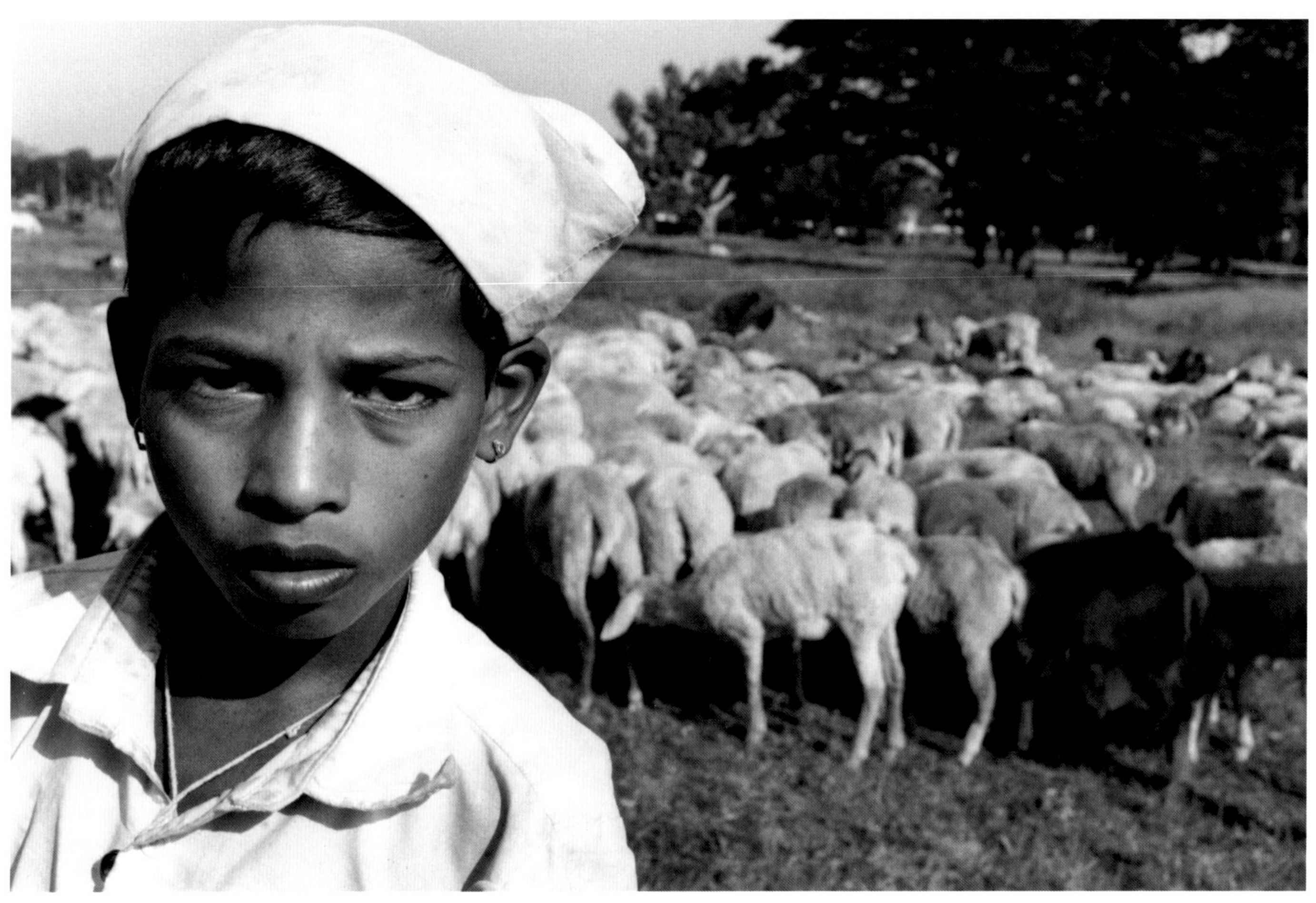

SANTANA
TAOS, NEW MEXICO

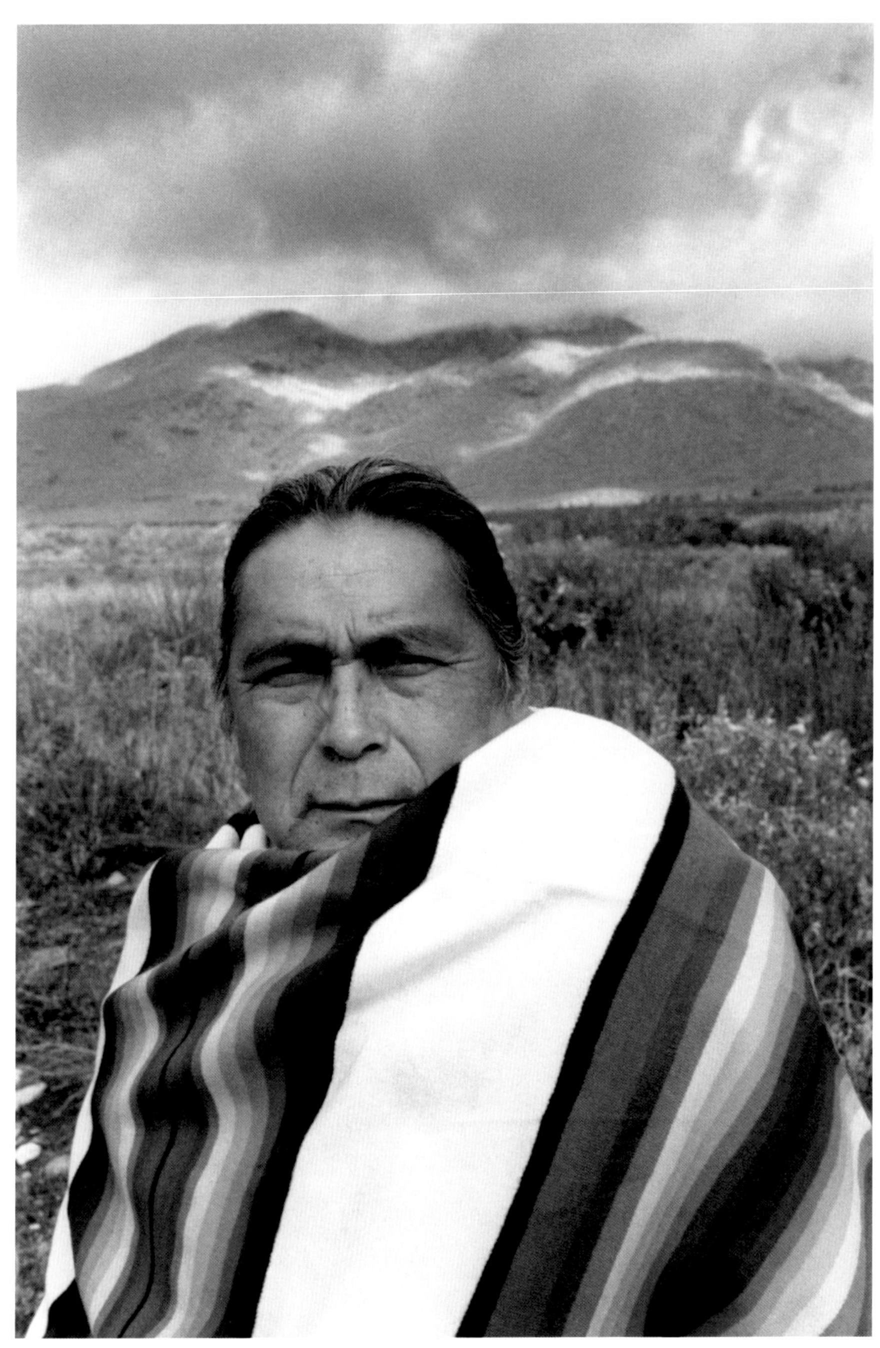

Margaret
Dungarvan, Ireland

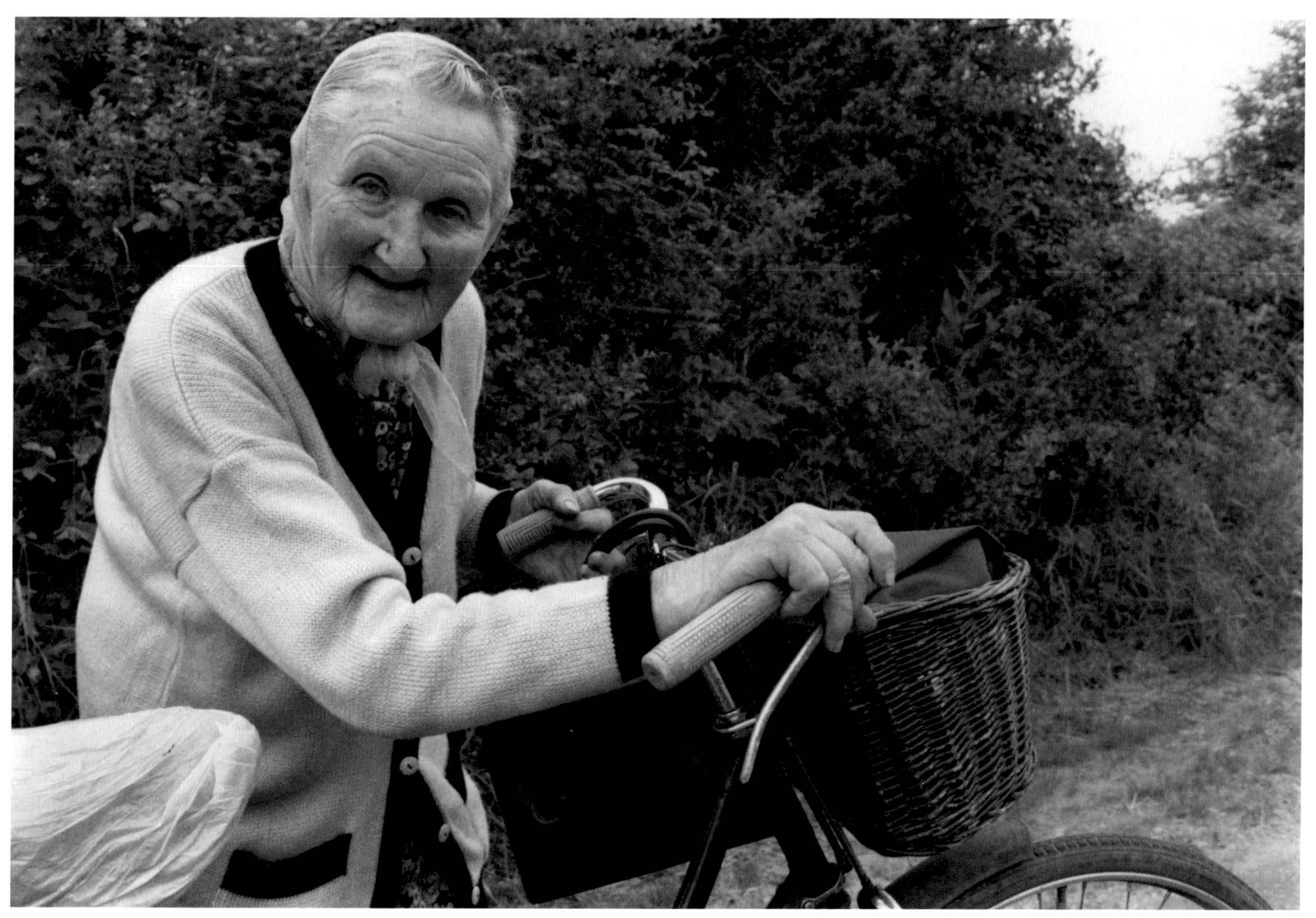

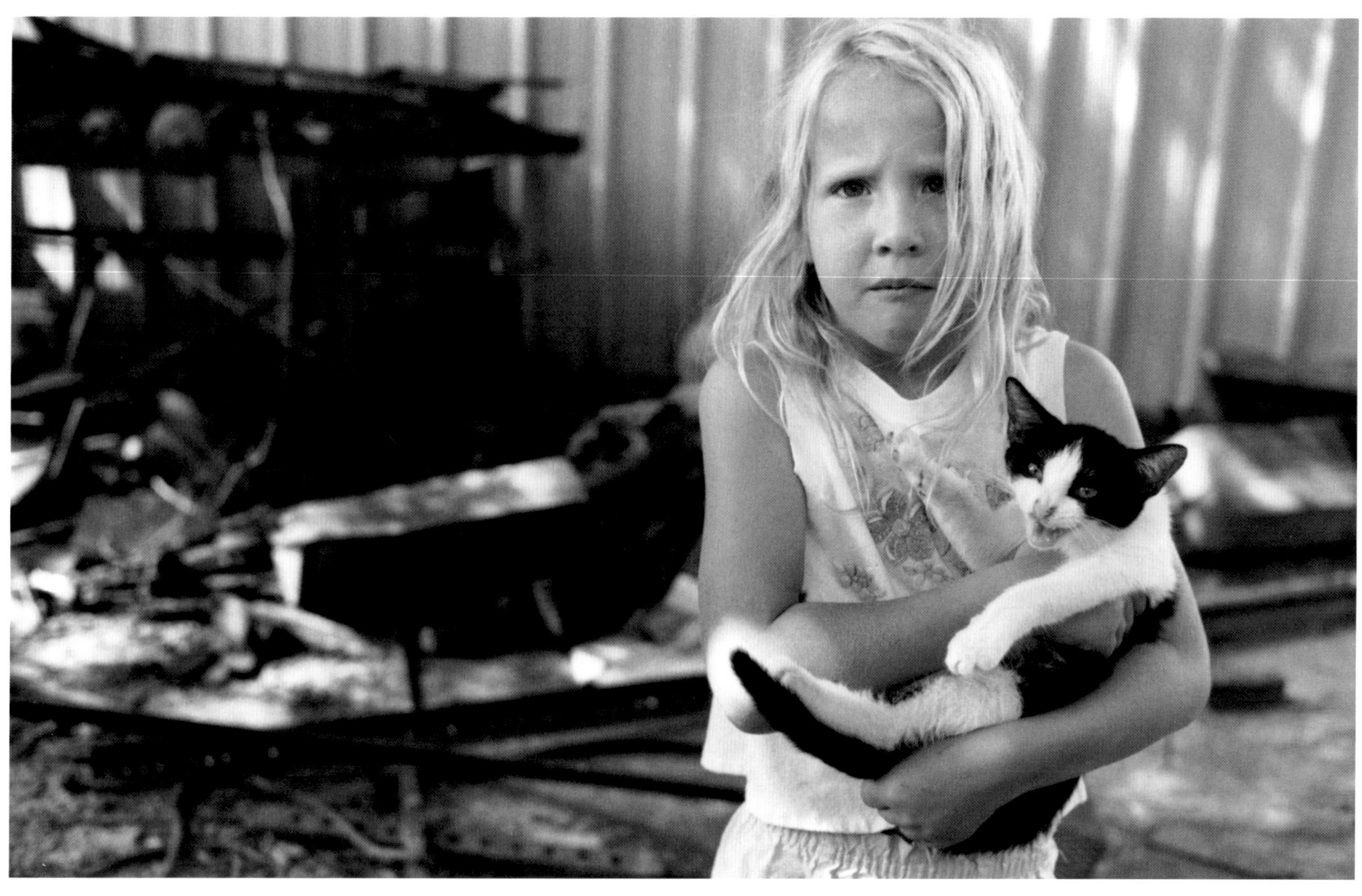

MIKE
TAOS, NEW MEXICO

31

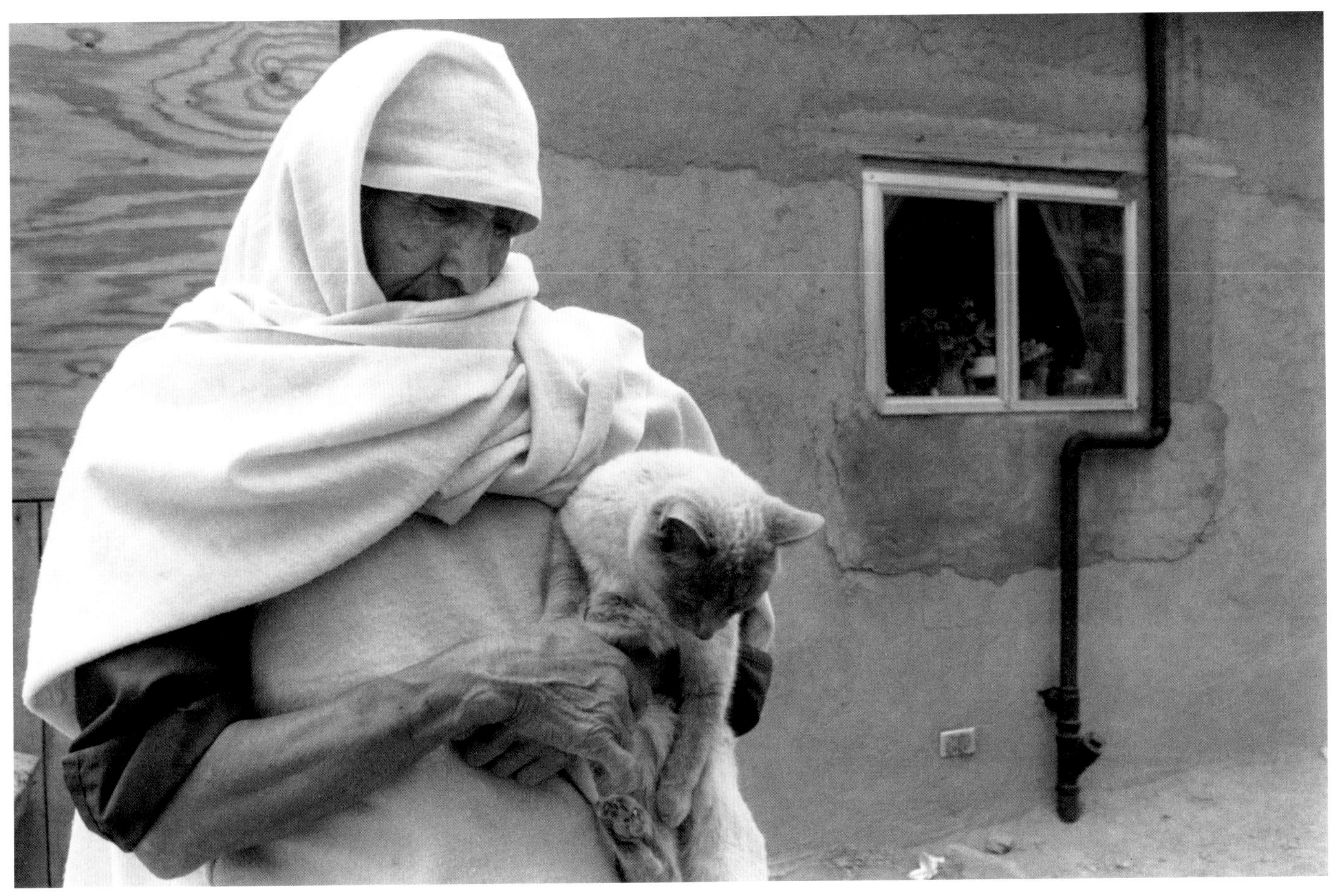

TRINIDAD, CUBA

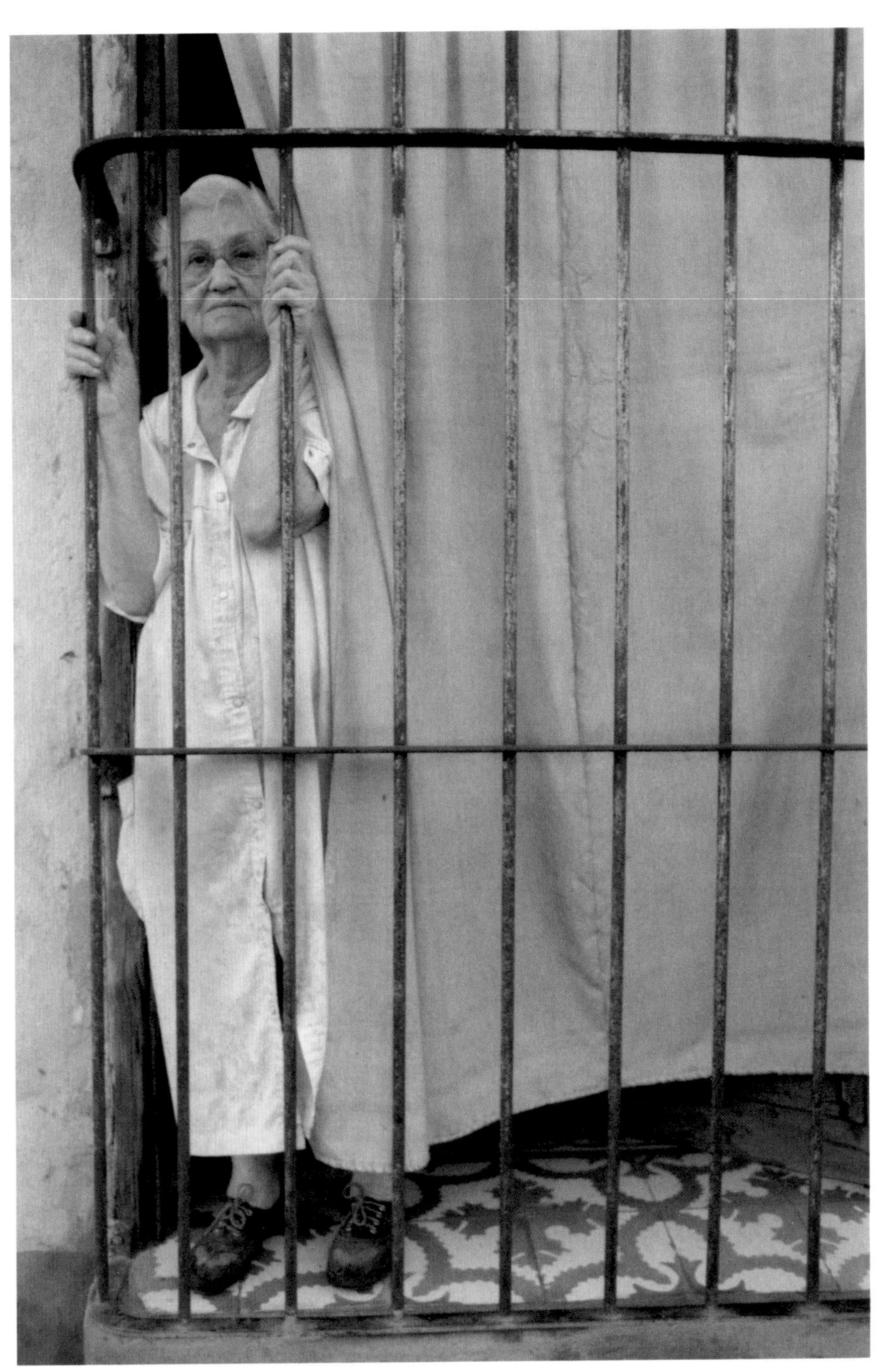

TURKEY-IRAQ BORDER

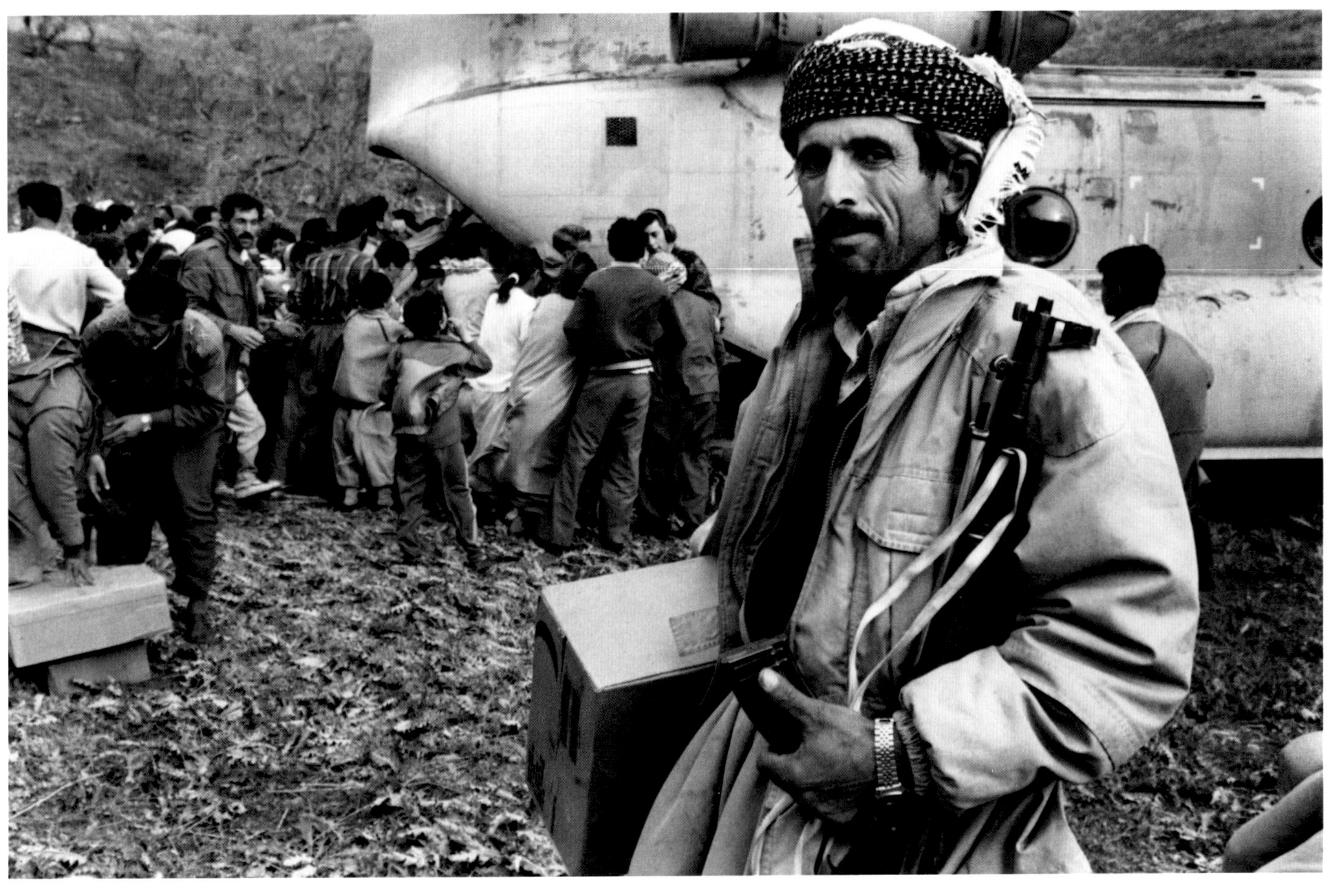

Ernesto
Taos, New Mexico

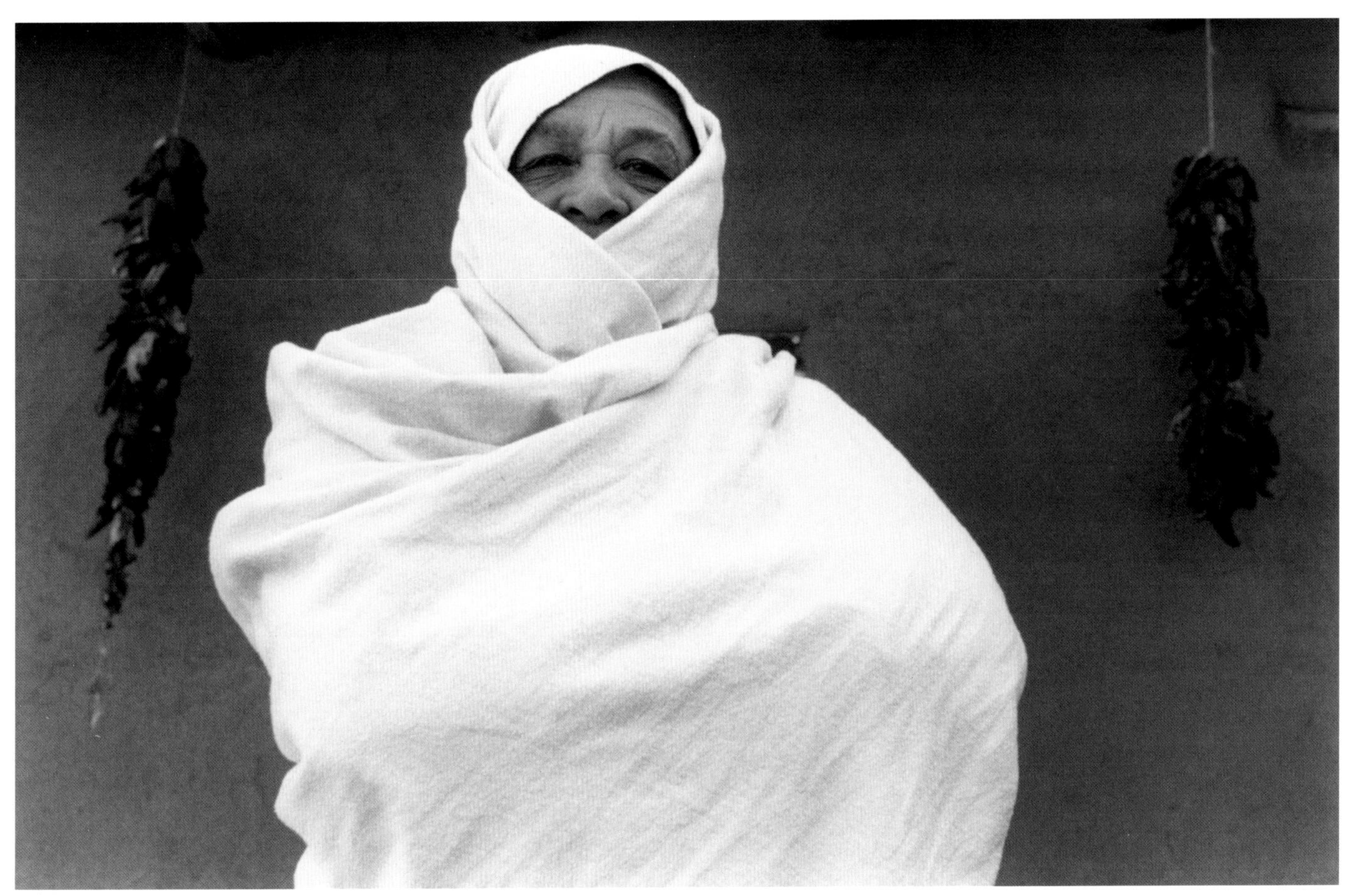

GEORGE
CATHOLIC BELFAST, IRELAND

35

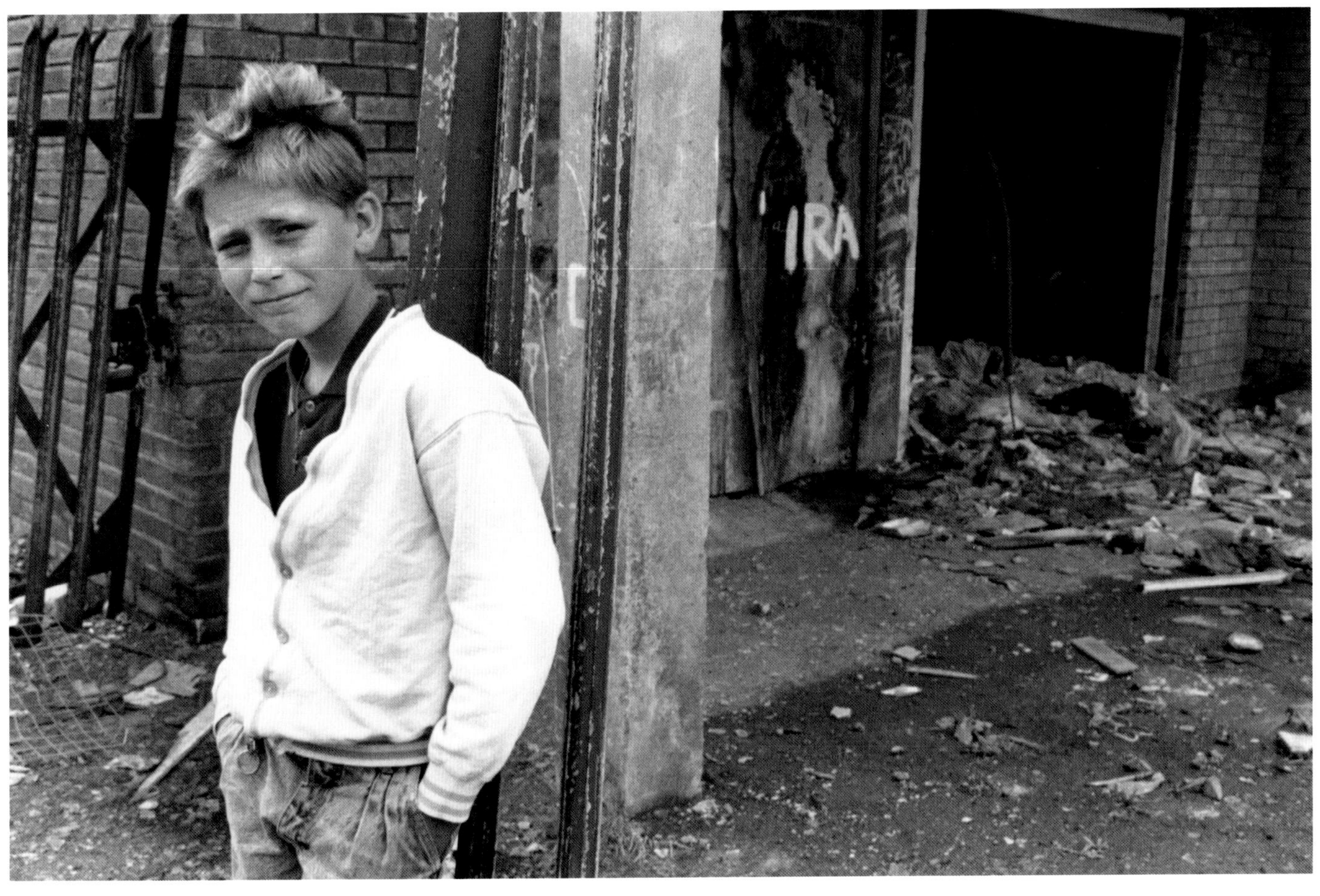
IRA

Jeremy & Spencer
Denver, Colorado

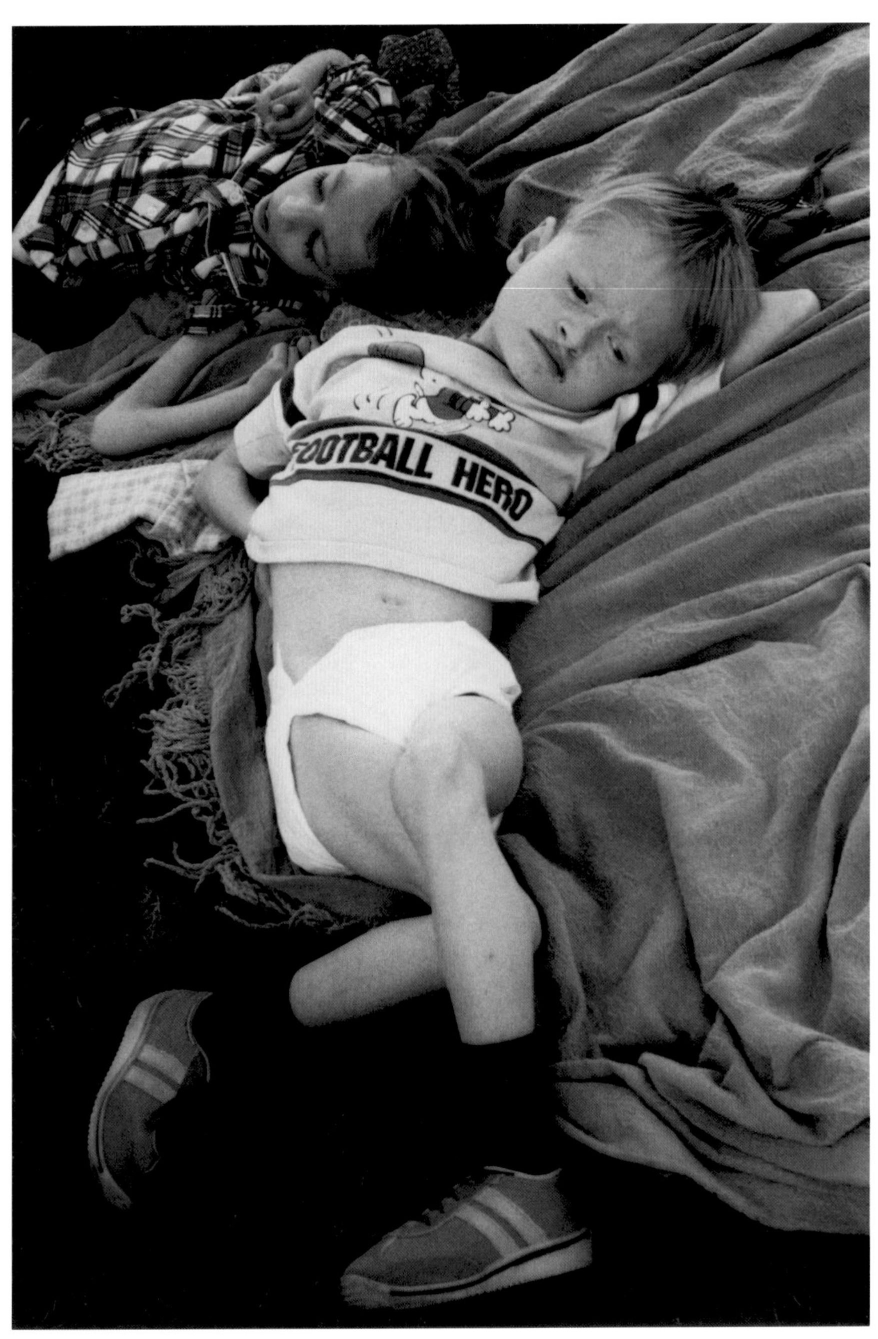
FOOTBALL HERO

TRINIDAD, CUBA

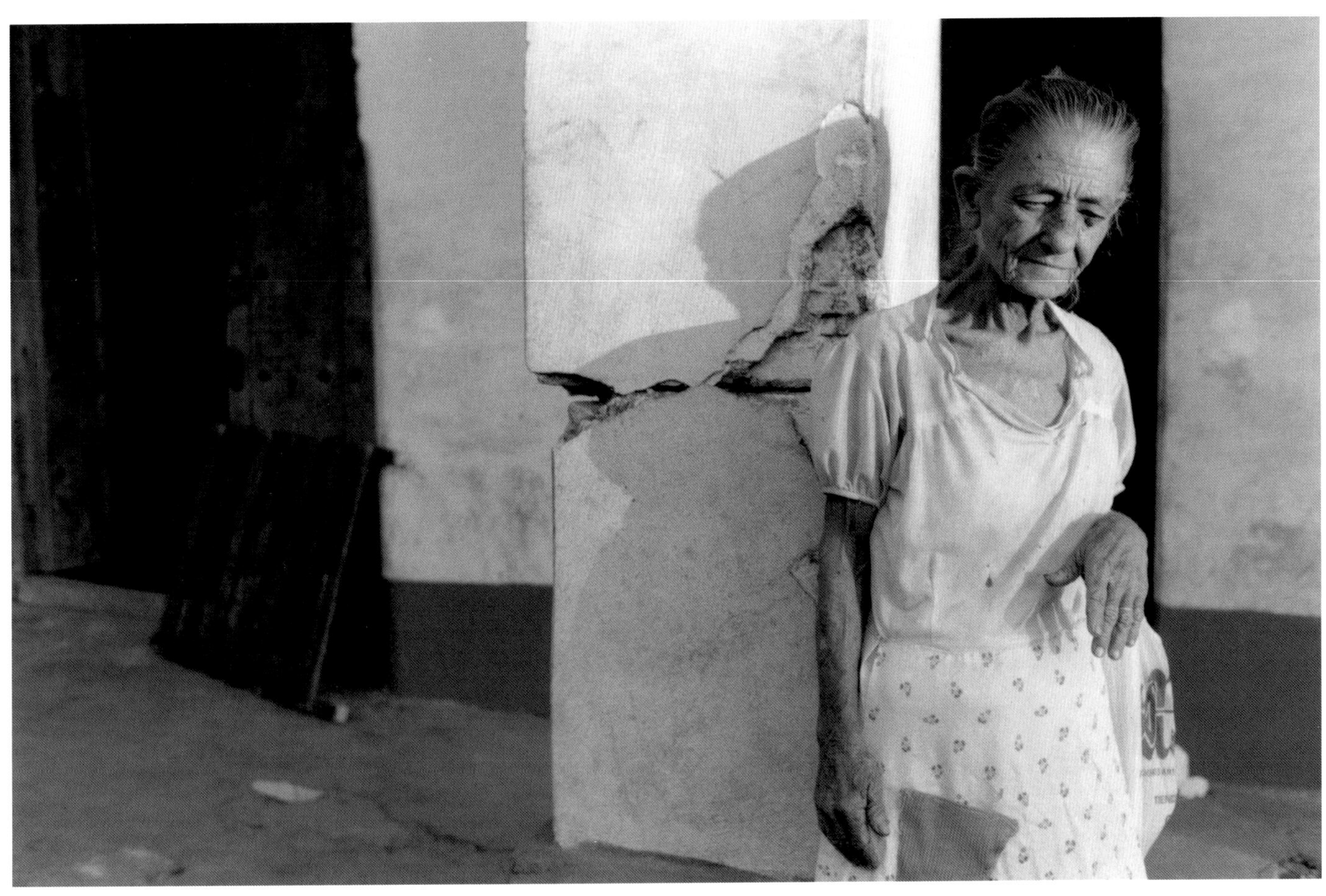

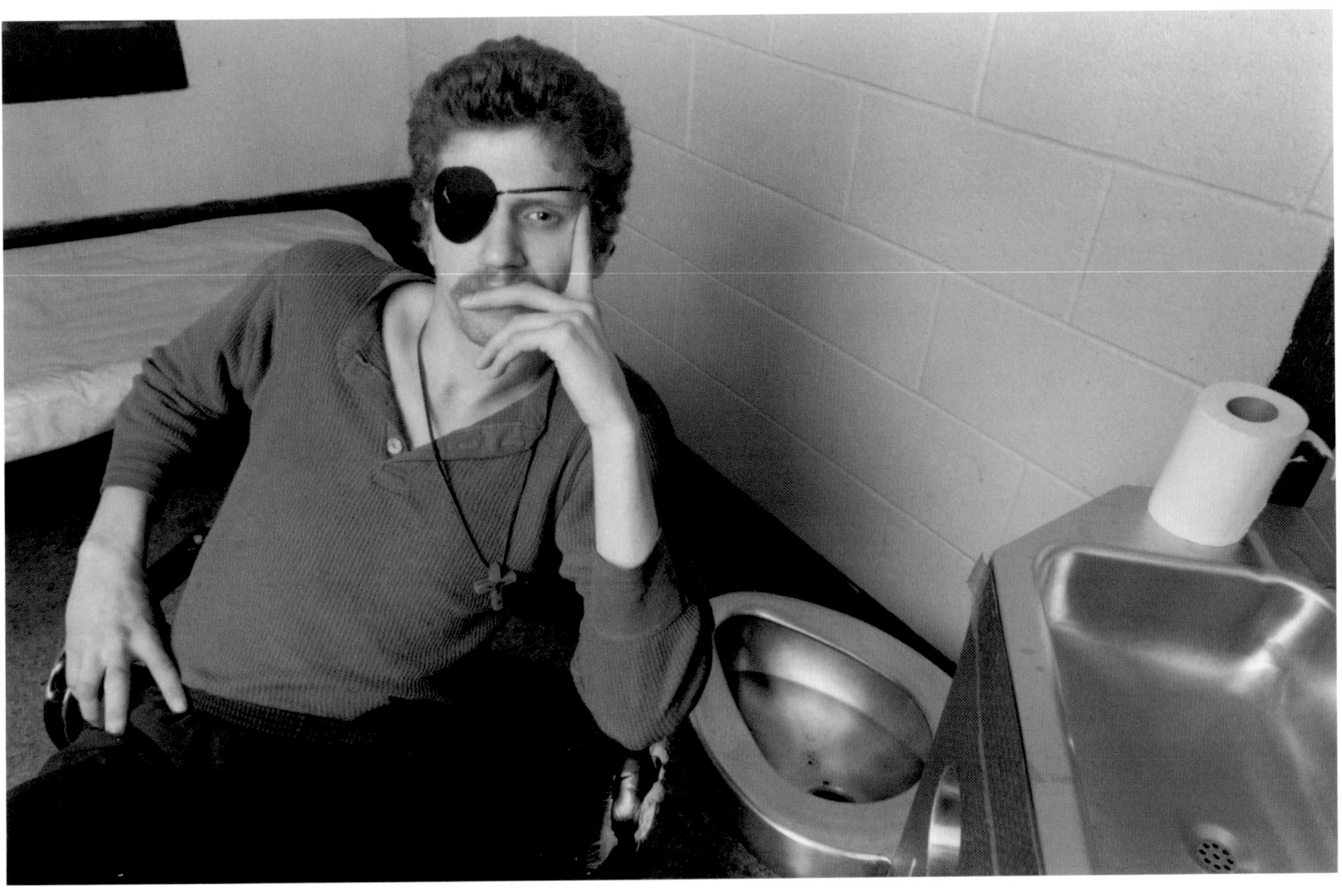

INSTITUTE FOR BLIND CHILDREN
PORT-AU-PRINCE, HAITI

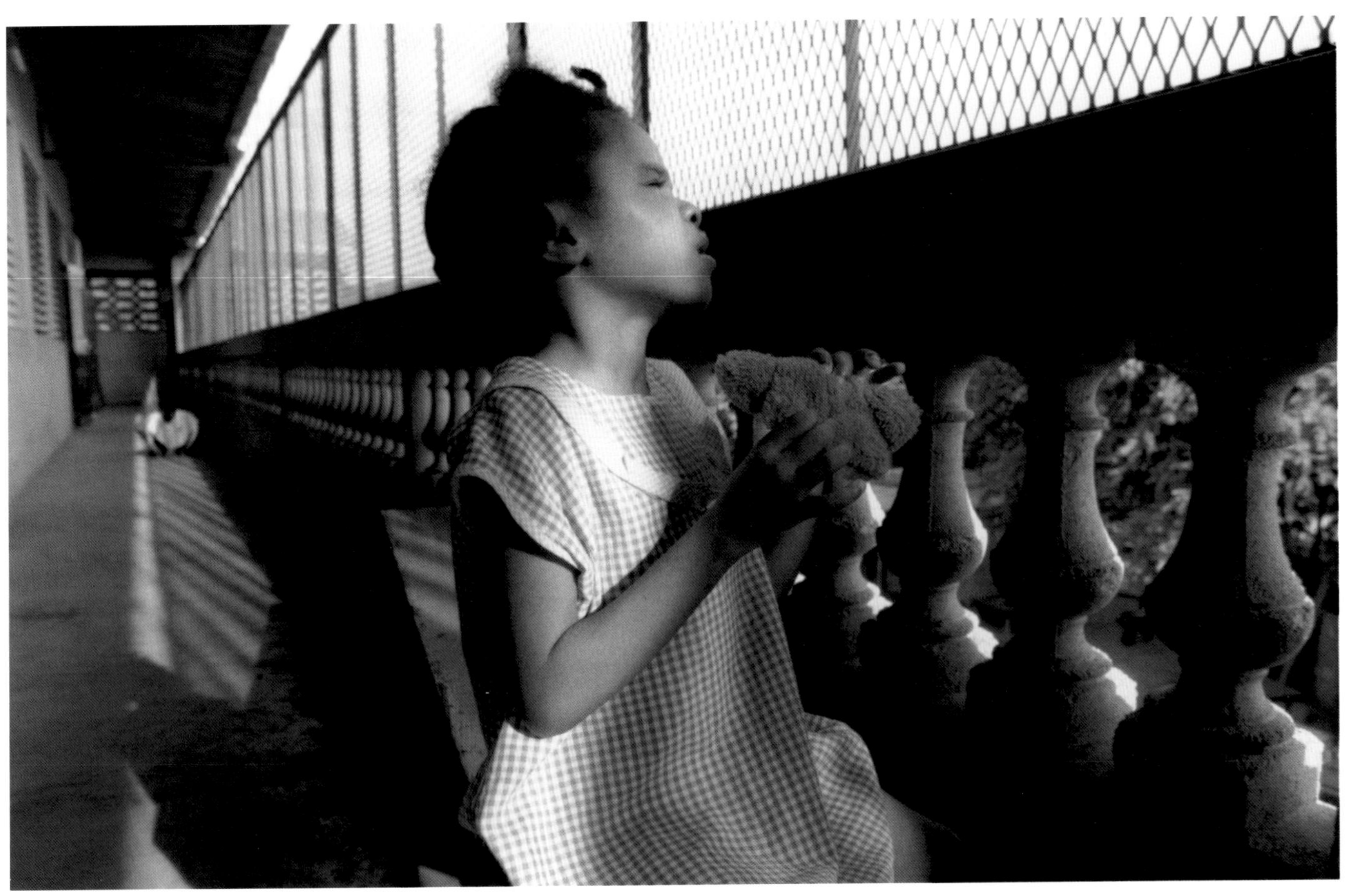

SIBERIA, RUSSIA

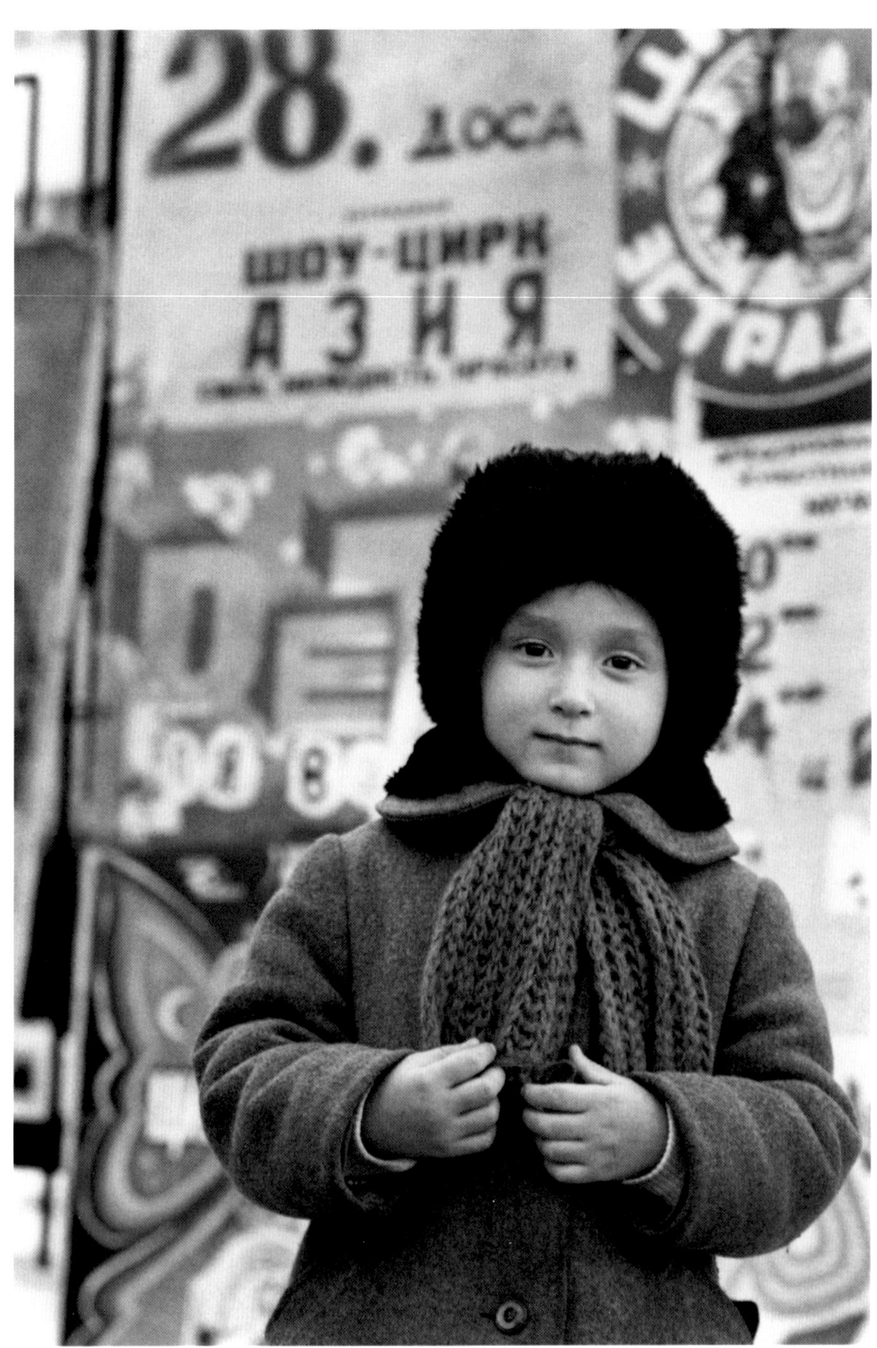
28. ДОСА
ШОУ-ЦИРК
АЗИЯ

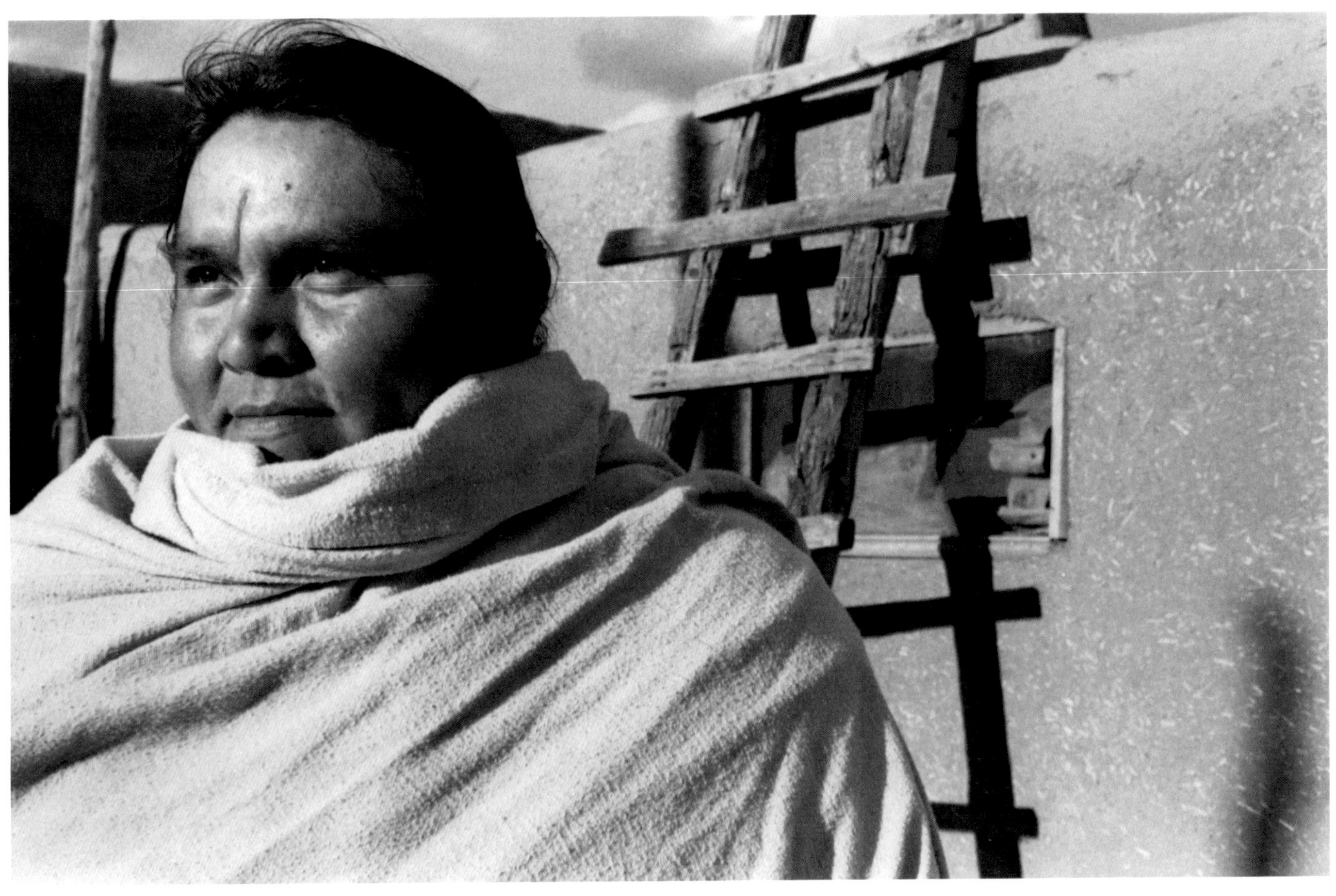

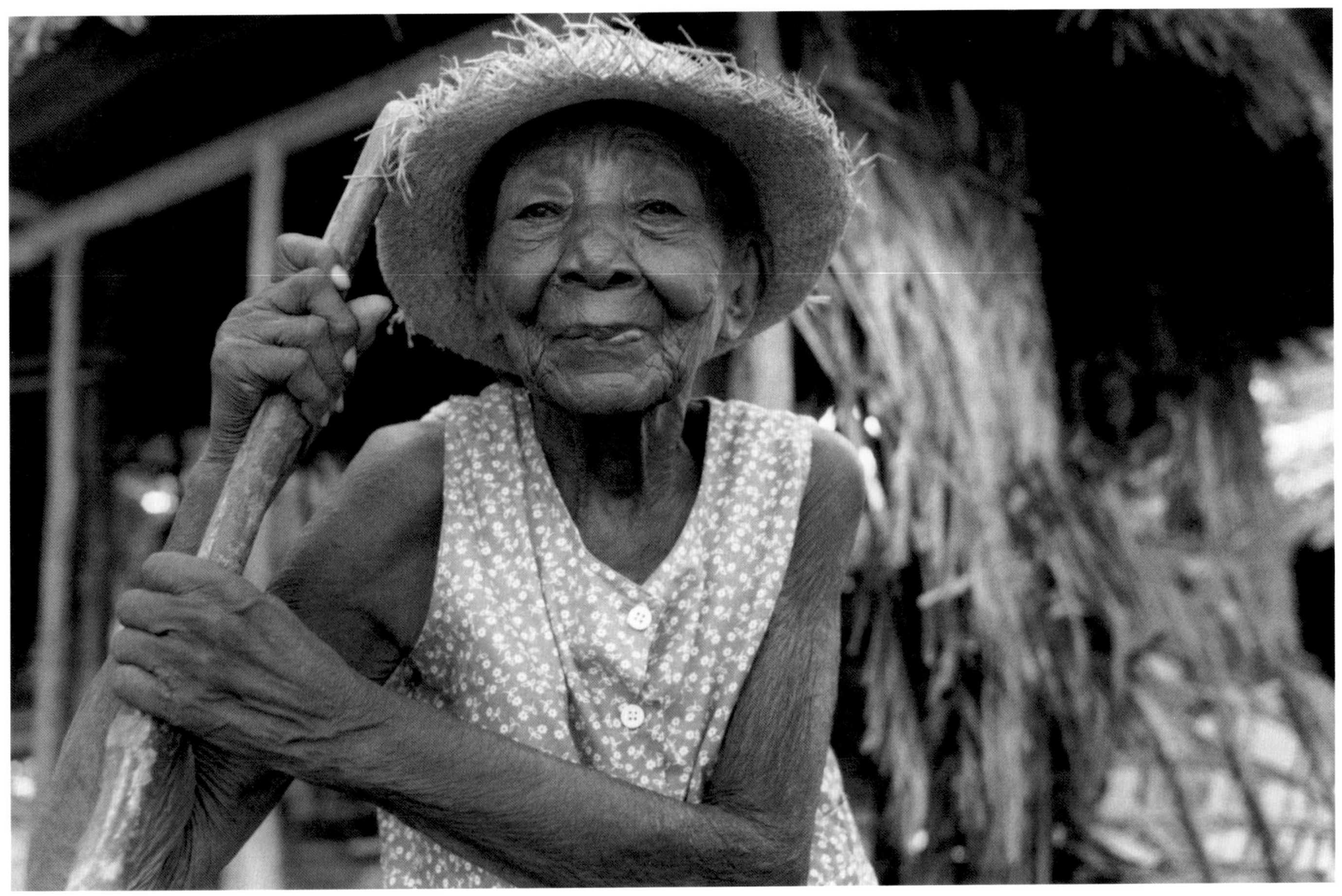

SOLOLA, GUATEMALA

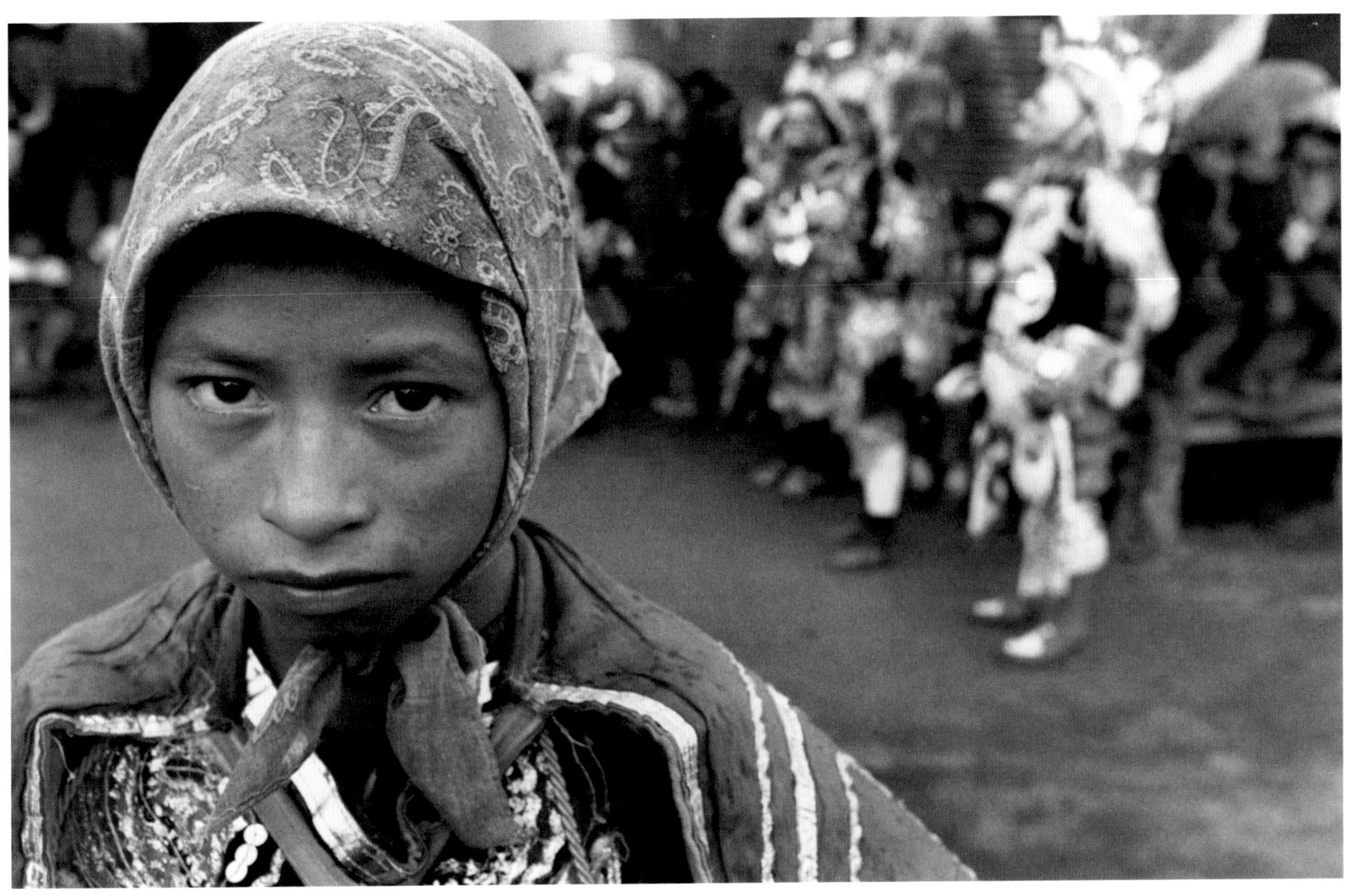

MARTINA
CATHOLIC BELFAST, IRELAND

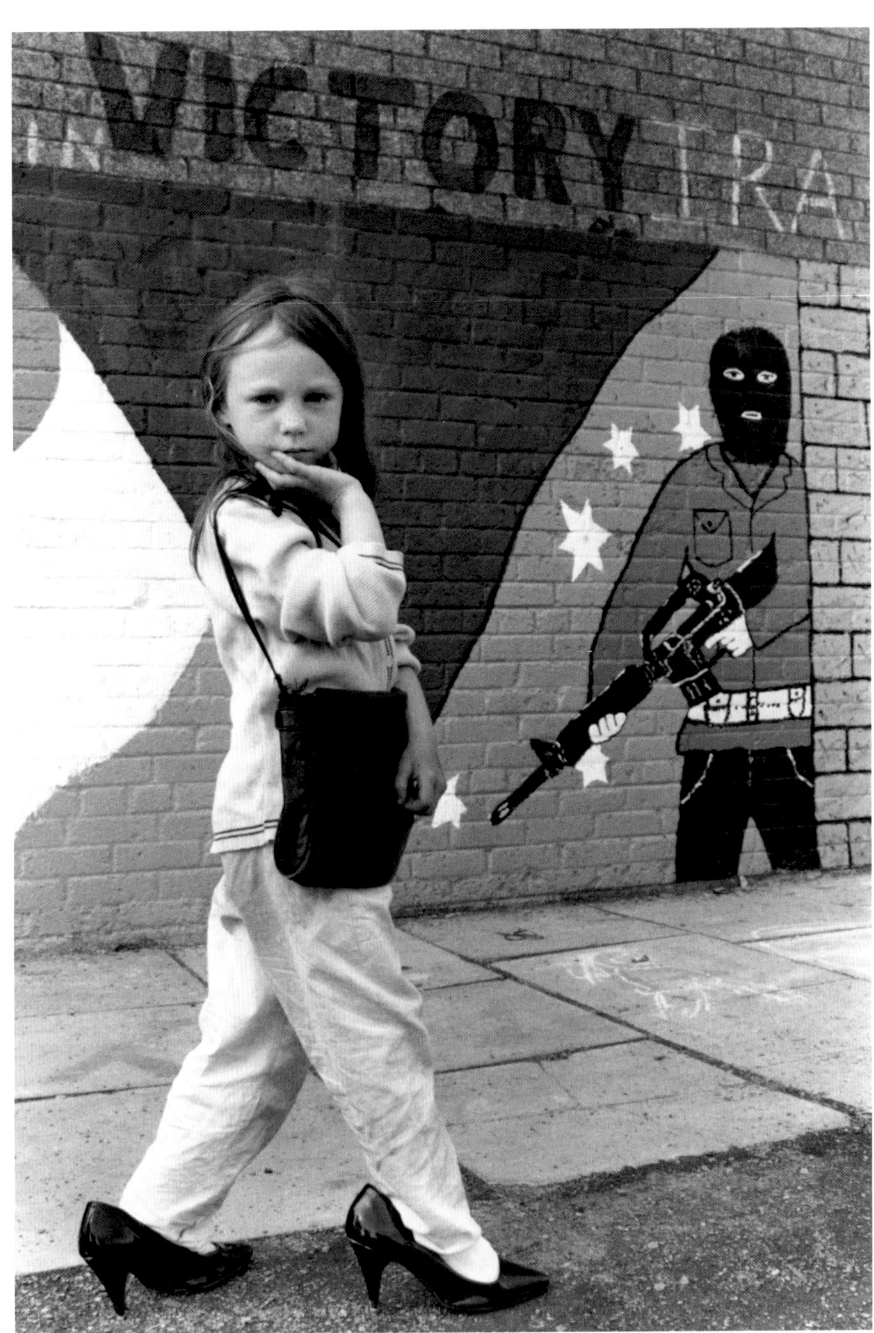
VICTORY
IRA

Antigua, Guatemala

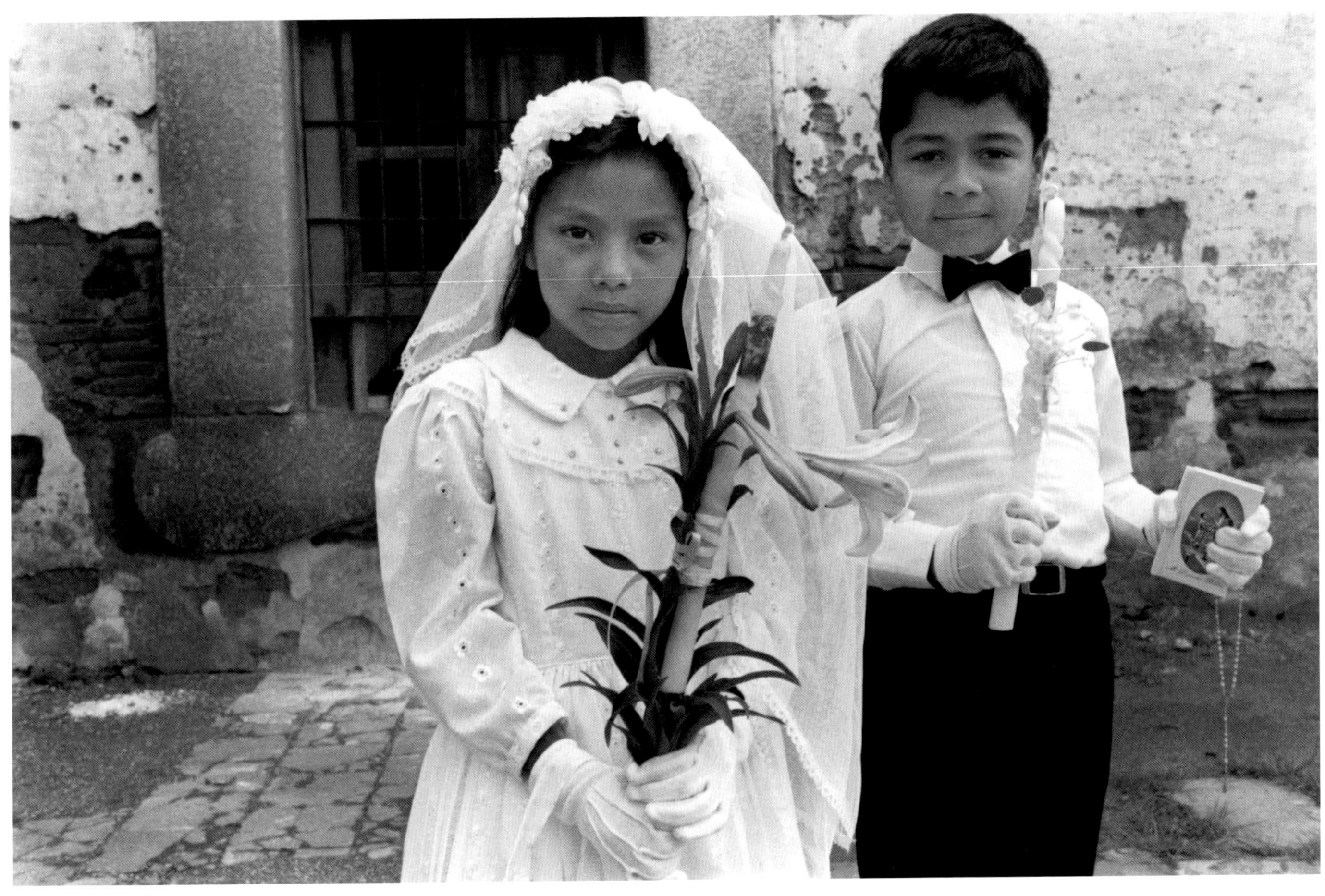

SANTO DOMINGO, DOMINICAN REPUBLIC

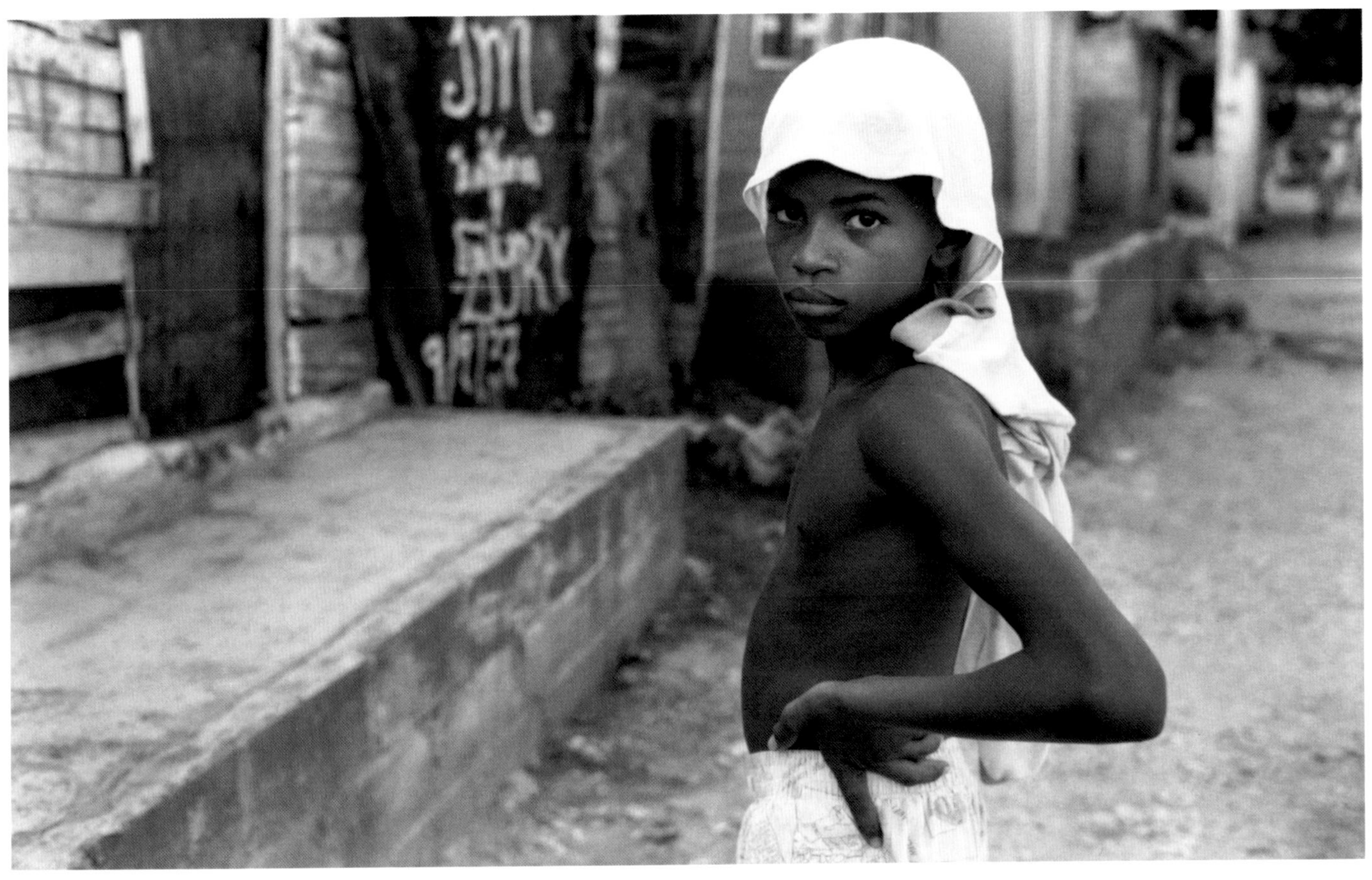

Gabriella
Helena, Arkansas

47

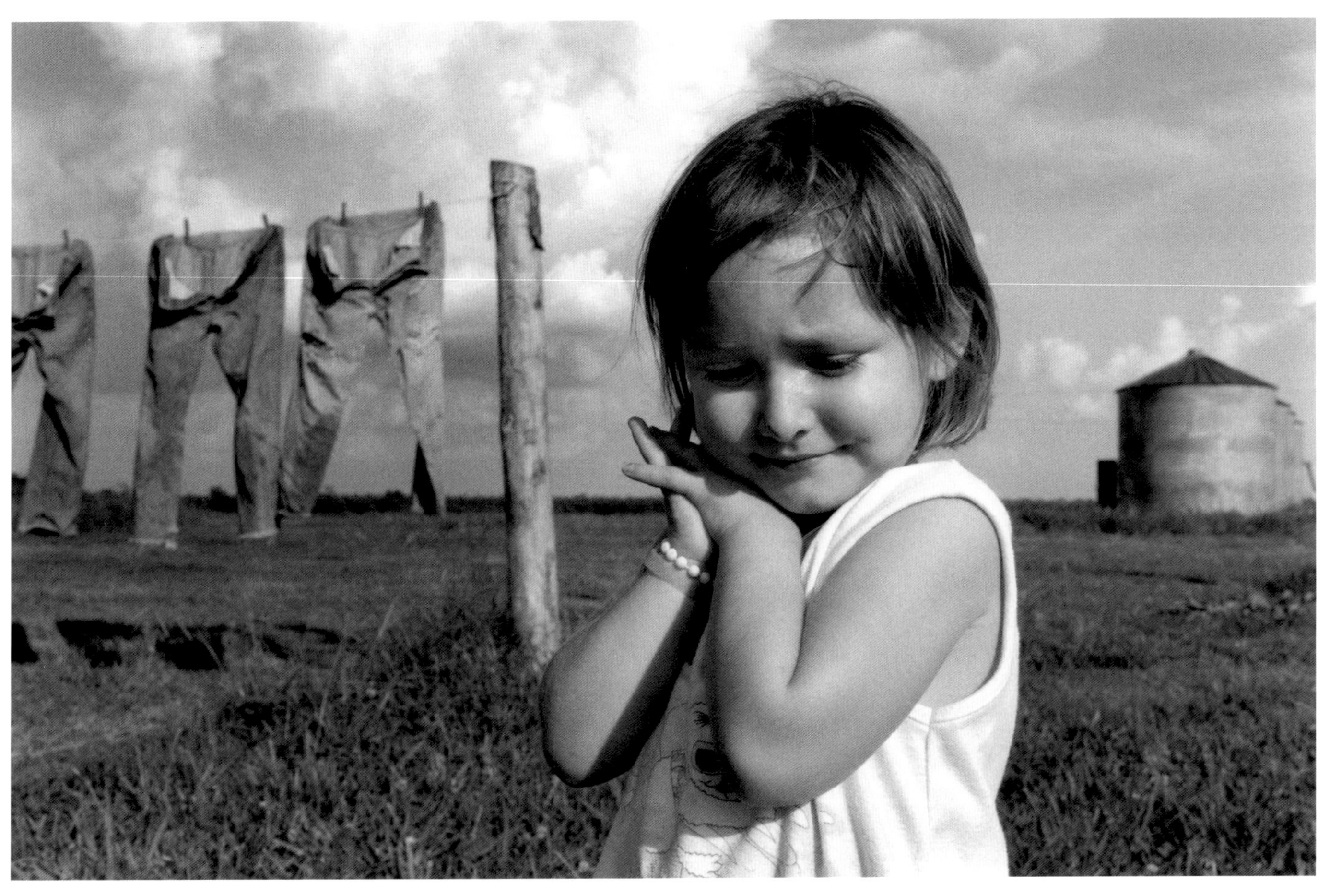

SEBASTIAN
KENT, CONNECTICUT

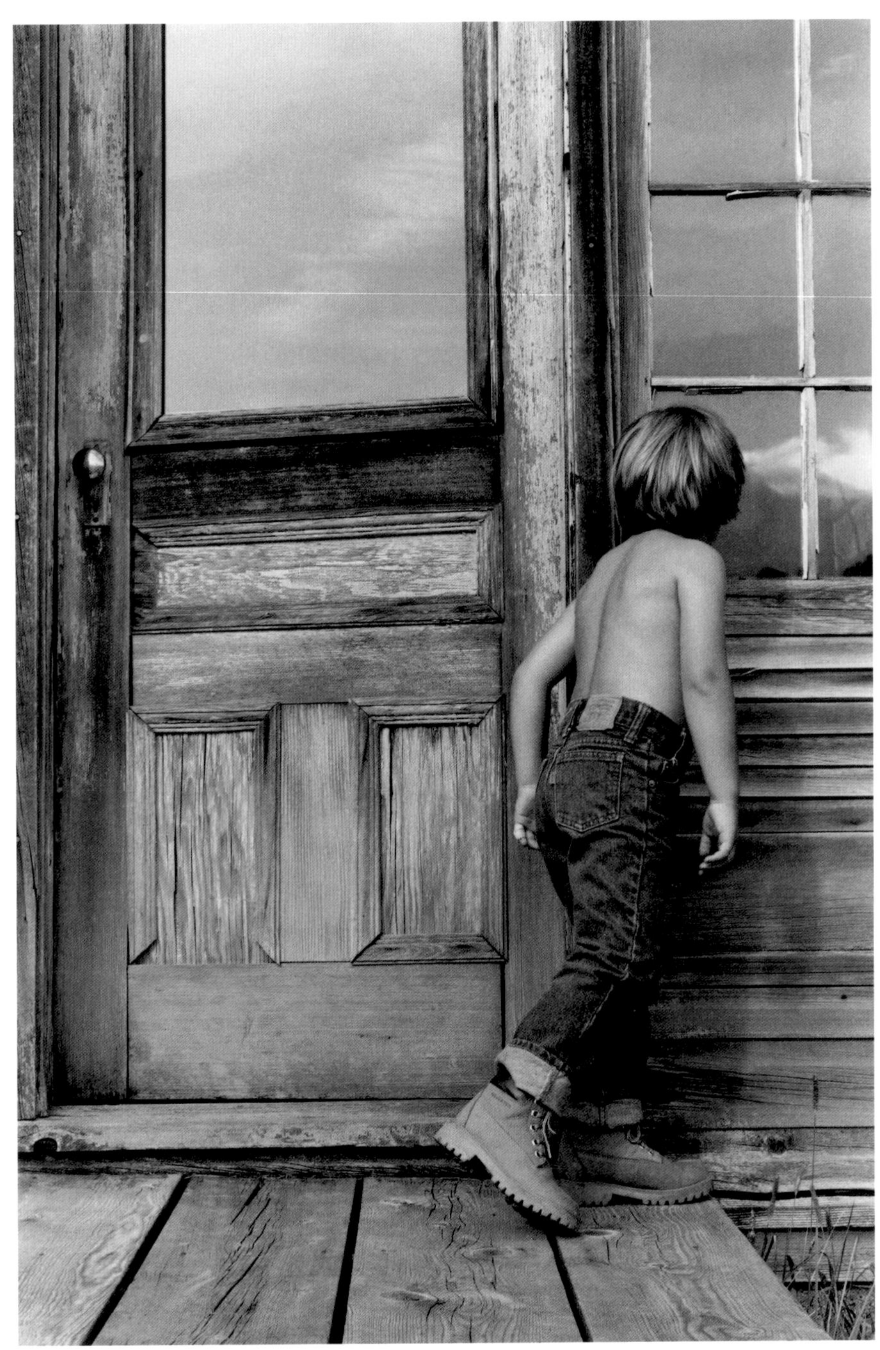